The Wreck of

THE EDMUND FITZGERALD

FREDERICK STONEHOUSE

Copyright 1977
ISBN 0-932212-88-3
Library of Congress No. 95-076479

By Frederick Stonehouse
and Avery Color Studos

First Edition — December 1977

Reprinted 1978

Updated Edition 1982

Reprinted 1982, 1983, 1984, 1985, 1986,
1987, 1988, 1989, 1990

Updated Edition 1991

Reprinted 1992, 1993, 1994

Updated Edition 1995

Updated Edition 1996

Reprinted 1996

Published by Avery Color Studios
Marquette, Michigan 49855

Printed by Lake Superior Press
Marquette, Michigan 49855

**Other Avery Color Studios books
by Frederick Stonehouse:**

Isle Royale Shipwrecks

Lake Superior's
Shipwreck Coast

Went Missing

Munising Shipwrecks

Keweenaw Shipwrecks

TABLE OF CONTENTS

THE FITZGERALD AT HER 1958 LAUNCHING

Photo Courtesey of the K.E. Thro Collection

*Does anyone know where the love of God goes
when the waves turn the minutes to hours?*

Gordon Lightfoot

INTRODUCTION

It has been written that fate was responsible for the wreck of the *Edmund Fitzgerald.* There will be theories that she was stolen by flying saucers, or that a magnetic abnormality broke her in two... and all sorts of nonsense. But in my opinion the purpose and goal of the historian is to find out what really happened. And it isn't fate, damn it. Fate does not come down and sink a ship.

In this book I have endeavored to present as accurate an historical account as possible of the sinking of the steamer *Edmund Fitzgerald*, the events leading up to her loss and the subsequent investigation. Much of the information is drawn directly from the final report of the Coast Guard Marine Board of Investigation. It isn't based on rumor, speculation or gossip. It is, as nearly as I could determine, the simple truth.

However, the sinking of that enormous carrier caused considerable stir and controversy. Even the Coast Guard's thorough and extensive investigation has come under fire. When the *Fitzgerald* disappeared from the radar screen of the trailing *Arthur M. Anderson* on November 10, 1975, it was an event that shook the Great Lakes maritime community. The attendant controversy, speculation and criticism can and should not be ignored. I have relegated my own opinions and personal feelings about the shipwreck to the book's final two chapters. In all that is written prior to that point, I tried to produce an objective and historically sound account.

November has traditionally been the worst time of year for storms on the Great Lakes. Over the years, November storms have been of truly hellish proportions and have taken a heavy toll of vessels and men.

A classic example was the notorious storm of November, 1913. When it finally died out, a dozen vessels were lost,[1] 16 vessels blown aground and approximately 254 sailors dead. A storm of similar severity struck in November of 1940, sinking five vessels and killing 67 men. November was cruel again in 1975.

I was in Marquette the night the *Fitzgerald* sank, and one could tell that it was going to be a bad night out on Superior. I went down to Presque Isle Park and watched the waves sweep over the island. From what I could see, it was one of the worst storms in years. I shot some 16 millimeter film of some of the waves sweeping over the breakwall and coming up the cove. I had never seen waves that large before.

People lulled by the false god of technology sometimes underestimate the awesome power of a Great Lakes Norther'. In the eighth decade of the 20th century, 729-foot steamers did not simply disappear. And when the *Fitzgerald* did, the news swept the nation. Radio, television and newspapers trumpeted the loss of the giant ore carrier. Less than a year after she sank, songwriter Gordon Lightfoot made it to the top of the popular music charts with a ballad entitled, *"The Wreck of the Edmund Fitzgerald."* [2]

Lightfoot's song, considering the information he had available at the time, was a pretty fair account. Others have been less scrupulous about sticking to the facts. A typical example of some of the nonsense being written appears in *The Great Lakes Triangle*, a book of "non-fiction" by Jay Gourley. Gourley laboriously attempts to include the *Fitzgerald* in a large list of ships and planes that disappeared in the Great Lakes area without any explanation:

". . . if the *Fitzgerald* had been in trouble, why hadn't the *Fitzgerald* reported it? The *Fitzgerald* had radios backed up by more radios — all designed for even the most improbable contingencies. The flip of a switch would have activated automatic battery-powered distress signals on several frequencies. There is nothing that can happen to a ship the size of the *Fitzgerald* so quickly that there is not time to flip a switch. No such transmissions were ever made. . ." [3]

People seem to *want* to believe such stuff. It's almost like a religion to them. But it's the historian's job to eliminate those alluring "mysteries." Rather than there being "nothing that can happen to a ship the size of the *Fitzgerald*," there are, indeed, *several* things that could have happened. This book will consider all of them.

The last major vessel lost on the Great Lakes due to storm was the steamer *Daniel J. Morrell.* She went down in November of 1966 in Lake Huron. The force of the storm broke the *Morrell* in two and she quickly sank, taking with her 28 of her 29-man crew.

Prior to that time, in November of 1958, the self-unloader *Carl Bradley* broke in two and sank in a Lake Michigan gale. Loss of life was again high; 32 of 34 men perished.

The last Lake Superior storm loss was the *Henry Steinbrenner* in May of 1953. Buffeted by 70 mph winds and 25-foot seas that eventually tore off several hatch covers, she sank 15 miles south of Isle Royale. She lost 17 men.

But those three vessels were relatively old craft. Their average age at time of loss was 47 years. The *Edmund Fitzgerald* was only 17 years old — an adolescent by Great Lakes standards! When she was launched on June 8, 1958, she was the largest ship on the Lakes. At the time of her wreck, she was considered sturdy, strong and apparently in good repair.

Facts such as these, however, have never meant much to Lake Superior — the Lake the sailors used to call "Old Treacherous." I have always believed Superior to be the roughest of the Lakes, even though other Lakes lose more ships. The other Lakes carry more traffic, and therefore offer more "targets" than does Superior, but from purely subjective experience in comparing gales I've seen on Superior and other Lakes, I'll say Superior's the roughest every time.

As a diver, I have enjoyed diving Superior more than any of the other Lakes. It's by far the cleanest and the clearest of the Lakes. It's also the coldest.

I think I can imagine what the *Fitzgerald* would be like for a diver. I've been down on several steel steamers, (although certainly on nothing approximating her size). Those steamers were pretty torn up, too, as a result of having gone down. I can picture the plates on the *Fitzgerald*. I can visualize the way they're torn. . . those popped rivets — Everything!

1. Stonehouse, Frederick. **Went Missing, 15 Vessels that Disappeared on Lake Superior.** Avery Color Studios, AuTrain, Michigan, 1977.
2. **The Wreck of the Edmund Fitzgerald,** Gordon Lightfoot, Moose Music, Ltd. 1976.
3. Gourley Jay, **The Great Lakes Triangle,** Fawcett Publications, Inc., Greenwich, Connecticut, 1977.

THE BELLE RIVER, one of the new breed of 1,000-foot super carriers, was launched in the fall of 1977. Capable of carrying cargo loads of nearly 60,000 tons, almost one and three quarters the combined weight of the *Fitzgerald* and her last cargo, the *Belle River* is a self-unloader carrying coal from the Duluth-Superior area to the lower lakes.

Mary George Photo

12

PRIDE OF THE AMERICAN FLAG

THE EDMUND FITZGERALD

The *Edmund Fitzgerald*, official number 277437, was built in 1958 as hull number 301 at the Great Lakes Engineering works at River Rouge, Michigan.

More than 10,000 people watched as the vessel slid into the water on June 8, 1958, christened by Mrs. Edmund Fitzgerald, wife of the president of the Northwestern Mutual Life Insurance Company.

The Fitzgerald family had long been involved with Great Lakes shipping. Edmund Fitzgerald's grandfather, John, skippered several vessels, as did John's five brothers.[1]

With an overall length of 729 feet and a gross tonnage of 13,632, she and her sister ship, the 13,390-ton Bethlehem Steel Corporation vessel *Arthur B. Homer*, became the largest carriers on the Great Lakes.[2] The *Fitzgerald* remained the largest ship on the Lakes until 1971.[3]

Proudly labeled "The Pride of the American Flag," the *Fitzgerald's* production cost had topped $8.4 million; to replace her in 1976 would have cost in excess of $20 million.[4]

Deep in her engine room rested a 7,000 horsepower steam turbine, capable of pushing the giant ore carrier at more than 16 miles per hour.

The *Fitzgerald* set numerous shipping records. In 1964 she became the first Great Lakes vessel to carry more than a million gross tons of ore through the Soo Locks.[5] In 1968 she topped that earlier record by hauling 1.2 million tons through the Locks. Her single trip record load was 27,402 gross tons in 1969.[6]

Although owned by the Northwestern Mutual Life Insurance Company of Milwaukee, she was under charter to the Columbia Transportation Division of the Oglebay Norton Company of Cleveland until 1983.

Like many lakers, the *Fitzgerald* was equipped for carry-

13

ing passengers as guests of the Company. Her last passenger voyage took place in 1975 just a few weeks before her loss.

The plush passenger accommodations consisted of two staterooms for four passengers and a large lounge. Stewards treated the guests to the entire VIP routine. The cuisine was reportedly excellent and snacks were always available in the lounge. A small but well-stocked kitchenette provided the drinks. Once each trip the captain held a candlelight dinner for the guests, complete with mess-jacketed stewards and a special "clamdigger" punch. [7]

In all respects, the *Edmund Fitzgerald* was a conventional "straight decker" Great Lakes ore carrier. Cargo holds were located in the center of the vessel. Ballast tanks were situated below and outboard of the holds. (In her final, ill-fated voyage, these ballast tanks may have sustained damage. In the investigation which followed her sinking, these tanks and theories concerning their possible flooding would occupy hours of the Marine Board's attention.)

The forward deckhouse contained both crew accommodations and the pilothouse. The after deckhouse contained crew accommodations and the mess room. Crewmen were able to travel between the two deckhouses across the open spar deck or through port and starboard access tunnels located above the cargo hold and below the open deck. A collision bulkhead was located between the forepeak and the forward ballast tank. There were watertight bulkheads forward and aft of the engine room.

If the controversy surrounding damage done to the ballast tanks was pointed, it was nothing when compared with arguments about the *Fitzgerald's* hatches and whether or not they were responsible for the ship going down.

There were 21 separate (11 foot by 48 foot) cargo hatches arranged on 24 foot centers down the midsection of the ship. Below the hatches were three cargo holds, separated by non-watertight screen bulkheads. Each hatch had a 24-inch high coaming surrounding the opening and a hatch cover consisting of a single piece of 5/16-inch steel fitted with a sealing gasket. Each hatch cover was secured by 68 manually operated "kestner clamps." [8] These double-pivot, adjustable tension clamps were arranged on approximately two-foot centers around the perimeter of the hatch. Each clamp had an adjustable bolt to increase or decrease the force required to secure it. The adjusted tension also regulated the amount of hatch cover deflection, gasket compression and general tightness of the hatch. There was no routine maintenance policy concerning either the clamps or gaskets. An electrically-powered hatch crane was used to remove and replace the hatch covers.

Additional access to the cargo holds was provided by two 30 by 60 inch hatches through the spar deck. One hatch was to the forward, or Number 1 hold. The other was to the aft or Number 3 hold. Doors through the screen bulkheads provided access to the center or Number 2 hold.

Eight ballast tanks were located outboard of and below the cargo holds. Two eight-inch vent pipes extended from each tank through the spar deck to a height of 18 inches. A "mushroom" closure cap was provided for each vent, but there was no visible indication whether the vents were open or closed. Similar vents were provided to the port and starboard access tunnels.

Two of these ballast tank vents were lost on the *Fitzgerald's* last voyage. At the time, their loss was reported by the ship's captain, the problem seemed minor. Later, the loss of the vents would be exhaustively scrutinized by investigators.

Manual sounding of the ballast tanks was possible by using sounding tubes on the weather deck and it was also possible to obtain a sounding report from remote reading gauges located in the engine room. There was no method available for determining the water level in the cargo holds. Soundings were usually recorded on special chalk boards called "sounding boards" located in the pilothouse and engineroom.

The ballast tanks were filled and drained by four electric 7000 gallon-per-minute main ballast pumps and two electric 2000 gallon-per-minute auxiliary pumps. These pumps could also be used to drain the Number 3 cargo hold through the ballast manifold and through the single suction well located in the Number 3 hold. As the cargo holds were "common", it was anticipated that water accumulating in the other holds would drain to the Number 3 hold where it could be pumped out.

When the holds were filled, water would have to seep through the cargo before it could be pumped out and many Great Lakes sailors have maintained that, because of the choking effect of cargo, the cargo holds could not be effectively pumped once the ship was loaded.

It is important to note that the *Edmund Fitzgerald* was very well outfitted with emergency electronic equipment. Electric power was provided by two 400-KW steam turbo generators and a 200-KW diesel auxiliary. There was also an automatic-starting, 30-KW generator for emergency lighting located on the poop deck. If the main generator were to stop, the emergency generator would automatically activate and provide vital illumination.

The *Fitzgerald* had three separate VHF/FM 25 watt marine radiotelephones on board; two operated from ship's power, the third run from rechargeable batteries. One of the ship's power VHF/FM's was a full duplex (two-way) dial radiotelephone. The *Fitzgerald* also had a 100-watt AM radio and a 50-watt AM emergency battery-powered set. Despite this considerable assortment of communications equipment, she was unable to get off a single distress message before she disappeared.

The *Edmund Fitzgerald* was also equipped with a radio direction finder and two surface scan radar sets, but, incredibly, she was not required to have any electronic sounding gear. She had no depth gauge and no fathometer. If the *Fitzgerald* had needed to determine the depth of the water in which she was travelling, she was expected to use a hand lead, simply a piece of lead attached to a length of line. The hand line is taken to the bow of the vessel, thrown out and depth is determined by counting the number of knots or line markings. [9]

The *Fitzgerald* remained virtually unchanged from her 1958 launching until 1969 when a diesel bow-thruster was installed. A recent development in lake shipping designed to improve in-port maneuverability, a bow-thruster is a large propeller mounted in a tube near the bow of a vessel. The use of bow-thrusters often eliminates the need for harbor tug assistance.

During her 1971-72 winter layup in Duluth, the *Fitzgerald* was converted from coal to oil, with the fuel tanks filling the space formerly occupied by the old coal bunkers. A firefighting system and a sewage holding tank were also installed at that time.

Although several "minor" structural problems were discovered during her 17 years of successful operation, nothing was ever discovered which proved serious enough to cause the ore carrier to be removed from service on the Lakes. During the 1969-70 layup period, additional vertical stiffening was done to the keelsons to correct a cracking problem and during the 1973-74 layup the problem came up again, but was corrected by welding. None of these problems were considered unusual or serious.

Just as any working vessel, the *Fitzgerald* suffered her fair share of accidental damages. In September of 1969 she grounded near the Soo Locks suffering hull damage. April, 1970, saw her in a collision with the *S.S. Hochelaga*. In September of that same year, she rammed a lock wall at the Soo. She struck lock walls again in May 1973 and June 1974. None of these accidents resulted in any damages which were considered overly serious or unusual.

During the sailing season, maintenance of the vessel was the responsibility of the crew. Both the Master and the Chief Engineer had authority to contract for minor repairs, although repairs costing more than a few hundred dollars had to be approved by the home office. While the vessel was in winter layup, repairs and maintenance were attended to by various contractors and a winter standby crew, provided for the entire fleet.

At the time of the *Fitzgerald's* loss, the winter work list for the ship had not yet been written up, although preliminary inspections had already been made. Company inspectors, testifying at the Coast Guard Marine Board hearings, insisted that the winter work list for the *Edmund Fitzgerald* would have been strictly routine. However, one of the major items to have been included on that list was repair to damaged hatch covers and coamings. Identical work had been done during previous layups. This item, although "routine" in the eyes of the company, would later become an important consideration in the Coast Guard's Marine Casualty Report.

The *Fitzgerald* carried two 50-man lifeboats and two 25-man life rafts. The life rafts were carried in special racks designed to allow them to float free and inflate on the surface. One was situated near the pilothouse, the other near the after deckhouse to allow full crew access.

According to regulation, the lifeboats and life rafts each had to be capable of carrying all the crew members. Because the ship had widely separated sleeping and working areas, one raft was required to be carried forward and the other aft, providing full access to the entire crew at all times.

There is no evidence that any of the lifesaving devices aboard the *Edmund Fitzgerald* were so much as touched by any of the crew before the giant ore carrier plunged to the Lake's bottom.

After the wreck, one lifeboat and a portion of the other were recovered off Coppermine Point. Only the forward 16 feet of the Number 1 lifeboat was found. The Number 2 lifeboat — *(pictured on the first page)* — was recovered whole but severely damaged. Her stem plating was fractured from the gunwale to the keel to the stem for some 12 feet on the port side and nine on the starboard side. The lifeboat had obviously been through a real struggle.

Testimony given by Great Lakes merchant mariners at the Coast Guard investigation has seriously challenged the effectiveness of such heavy lifeboats in the kind of weather encountered by the *Fitzgerald*. The mariners who testified didn't believe that such boats could even have been launched in the heavy sea of November 10, 1975. One Great Lakes pilot testified, ". . . I have said that if the damn ship is going down, I would get in my bunk and pull the blankets over my head and say, 'Let her go,' because there is no way of launching the boats." [10]

On vessels such as the *Fitzgerald*, the Coast Guard requires that fire and lifeboat drills be held a minimum of one time each week. In the instance of the *Fitzgerald*, this regulation was apparently not adhered to. Although licensed officers who had previously served aboard the *Fitzgerald* testified that such drills were conducted regularly, unlicensed sailors serving during the same period testified that they were not. Extracts from the *Fitzgerald's* log and the engineering log, both kept in the company offices, indicated only 14 drills for a 28-week period from April 12 to October, 1975; an average of only one drill every two weeks, half the required number.

The *Fitzgerald* carried more than the 83 life preservers required by regulation. She also carried 24 30-inch ring lifebuoys, 12 equipped with waterlights. There is no evidence that there was time to do more than think about any of the safety equipment, much less put it to use, on the night of November 10, 1975.

Dockside drills indicated that a lifeboat could be launched in approximately 10 minutes. It was estimated that 30 minutes would have been required for launching in any type of seaway.

It is interesting to note that most mariners had more confidence in the life rafts which were carried aboard Great Lakes vessels despite the fact that virtually none of those testifying at the Coast Guard Marine Board hearing had ever seen one inflated! Strangely, Coast Guard Regulation did not require life raft training.

Ocean vessels are required to carry an emergency position indicating radiobeacon (EPIRB), but Great Lakes vessels are not, and the *Fitzgerald* had none on board.

The load line requirements, (the level to which a ship may be filled with cargo), for Great Lakes vessels and those for ocean-going vessels of similar dimension are nearly identical. One critical difference, however, is that the longitudinal strength of the "laker" is only about half that of the ocean-going "salty."

From her 1958 launching until her loss, the load line requirements on the *Fitzgerald* changed several times. Her original winter requirements called for a level of 14 feet 9¼ inches freeboard. At the time of her loss, those winter standards had been relaxed to 11 feet 6 inches. In other words, she carried considerably more cargo and rode lower in the water than had been judged to be safe in 1958, her maiden year on the lakes.

Great Lakes "straight deckers" such as the *Edmund Fitzgerald* have a high degree of inherent stability, due primarily to the density of the iron ore (taconite pellet) cargo. One cubic foot of hold space usually contains about 130 pounds of taconite pellets. The stability generated by the sheer weight of the taconite cargo has, to the Coast Guard's way of thinking, exempted such carriers from stability tests and calculations. Moreover, Coast Guard regulations do not require general service cargo ships on either the Great Lakes or the oceans to meet any damage stability standards.[11]

The taconite pellet cargo is a remarkable product of our technological age. The pellets are manufactured by a process known as "oxide pelletizing" which begins with the mining of taconite, a low grade iron ore. The ore is crushed and ground while the iron is oxidized and waste materials removed. The remaining iron ore concentrate (in powder form), is dehydrated to about 10% moisture content and rolled into marble-sized balls, about one half inch in diameter. The pellets are then fired in a kiln at a temperature of 2200°F. to 2400°F., releasing still more moisture. The reddish brown pellets are then cooled and shipped. The *Edmund Fitzgerald* was bound for Detroit with 26,116 tons of these pellets (enough to produce approximately 7,500 automobiles) when she plunged to the bottom of Lake Superior.

Responsibility for loading and unloading cargos of taconite pellets is usually that of the Chief Mate. He is assisted by deck officers and crewmen. Information relating to the loading and unloading of cargo is carefully recorded and is frequently used as a reference with respects to loading sequence and quantity.

When a ship comes into dock at any loading facility, the cargo is not put aboard haphazardly. A very definite loading procedure is followed. For example, loading may progress at the Number 1 hatch and proceed aft, loading through parallel hatch covers, maintaining the trim of the vessel. Water used as ballast for an upbound passage is usually pumped out during loading so that when loading is complete, no water ballast remains aboard.

An ore carrier such as the *Fitzgerald* is loaded in one of two manners; either by a conveyor belt system or by chutes lowered to the ship from the more conventional ore dock. Conveyor systems are in use at Escanaba, Michigan and at the Reserve Mining Company dock at Silver Bay, Minnesota. Typical "ore docks" are used at Superior , Wisconsin and at Marquette, Michigan.

Photo Courtesy of Larry Van Dusen

An ore dock is equipped with storage bins ("pockets") constructed into the dock. Special chutes direct the ore or other bulk cargo from these pockets into the hatches of the loading vessel. Each ore dock pocket contains from 100 to 300 tons of taconite pellets. The vessel is normally shifted along the length of the dock to line up with new chutes during loading. The *Fitzgerald* frequently loaded at such dock facilities.

It usually required about five days for the *Fitzgerald* to complete a round-trip from Superior, Wisconsin to Detroit, Michigan. She might make as many as 47 such trips per season, although her ports of destination could vary. Loading usually took about four and a-half hours. Unloading usually averaged from 12 to 14 hours. [12]

The last inspection of the *Fitzgerald* was a spar deck inspection conducted at Toledo, Ohio on October 31, 1975. Coast Guard guidelines require that this inspection be conducted yearly during the shipping season.

Inspections are normally carried out during the winter layup period, but during layup, Great Lakes vessels are usually operating on shore power and have only a single watchman on board. To remove the hatches (which may be covered with snow or ice during the winter), would require the ship's power to be activated and the assistance of additional crewmen. Therefore, these spar deck inspections are conducted during the operating season while the vessel is loading or unloading. Only during actual loading and unloading activity is there enough personnel and power to carry out a thorough inspection.

The *Fitzgerald's* October 31 inspection revealed damage at four hatches. Gouges and cracks were found in the area of the hatch openings. Inspectors considered the damage routine — the natural result of a season's impact from dockside offloading equipment. The *Fitzgerald* was granted permission to operate with the stipulation that repairs be made to the damaged hatches prior to the 1976 shipping season. Ten days after that ruling there would be no *Fitzgerald* to repair.

1. **Milwaukee Journal,** Milwaukee, Wisconsin, November 13, 1975.
2. Wolff, Julius F., "One Hundred Years of Rescues of the Coast Guard on Lake Superior." **Inland Seas,** Spring, 1976.
3. Ibid.
4. Ibid.
5. **Milwaukee Journal,** Milwaukee, Wisconsin, November 13, 1976.
6. **Toledo Blade,** Toledo, Ohio, November 11, 1975.
7. **Toledo Blade,** Toledo, Ohio, November 17, 1975.
8. U.S. Coast Guard Marine Board of Investigation Report No. USCG 16732/64216, 10 November, 1975, Issued 1977. p. 5.
9. Ibid. p. 9
10. Ibid. p. 66
11. Ibid. p 76

A 36-FOOT MOTOR LIFE BOAT of the type stationed at Grand Marais, Michigan until replaced by a 44-footer in 1976, has been the mainstay of the Coast Guard life saving effort since the 1930's. The 36-footer is constructed of wood, is round-bottomed, self-righting, self-bailing and capable of a speed of 9 knots. This type of craft was standard equipment for search and rescue work under heavy sea and surf conditions.

Photo Courtesy of U. S. Coast Guard

LAST TRIP

In the early morning of November 9, 1975, the *Edmund Fitzgerald* was docked peacefully at Burlington Northern Railroad Dock No. 1 at Superior, Wisconsin, awaiting a routine trip to Detroit, Michigan. By 2:15 p.m. she had been loaded with 26,116 long tons of taconite pellets and was fueled for the voyage. ". . . crewmembers were observed replacing the hatch covers. There were no unusual incidents or occurrences and this appeared to be a routine loading and departure."[1]

About two hours later, in the vicinity of Two Harbors, Minnesota, she caught sight of the *Arthur M. Anderson*. The 767-foot *Anderson*, also carrying a cargo of taconite pellets, was downbound from Two Harbors for Gary, Indiana. The *Anderson* was separated from the *Fitzgerald* by 10 to 20 miles as the two steamers proceeded eastward along similar routes.

Meanwhile a storm, generated over the Oklahoma Panhandle on November 8, was proceeding northward on a historic journey of its own. Described originally by a National Weather Service forecaster as a "typical November storm," [2] it gathered forces rapidly as it roared over east central Iowa, headed for Wisconsin. By 7 p.m. on November 9, the National Weather Service had issued gale warnings for all of Lake Superior.[3]

Gale warnings were escalated to storm warnings in the early hours of November 10.

Shortly after 7 a.m., the *Fitzgerald* contacted the company office and indicated a delayed arrival at the Soo Locks because of the worsening weather conditions. At this time the storm's center had passed over Marquette, Michigan and was headed across Lake Superior.

Due to the intensity of the storm, the *Fitzgerald* abandoned the normal shipping lane along the southern shore and proceeded toward the northeast, about halfway between Isle Royale and the Keweenaw Peninsula. The *Fitzgerald* swung eastward, following the north shore and continuing southeastward along the eastern shore. By 1 p.m., November 10, she was 11 miles northwest of Michipicoten Island.[4]

The *Fitzgerald's* course change to the Lake's northern waters followed an old tradition born in the early days of steam navigation. This was the popular "fall north route" which offered more protection from prevailing northerly gales. The south route was much shorter, but was much more exposed and dangerous in a gale.

The *Fitzgerald* passed west of Michipicoten's West End Light and altered course to pass north and east of Caribou Island. Sometime after 7:15 p.m. something happened. In what seemed but a matter of seconds, the *Edmund Fitzgerald* disappeared.

What little knowledge we have of the *Fitzgerald's* last moments on the Lakes has been pieced together from the testimony of the officers and crew of the *Arthur M. Anderson.*

Shortly after joining the *Fitzgerald* off Two Harbors, the *Anderson* received notice of the gale warnings. Sometime after 2 a.m. on November 10, Captain Jesse B. Cooper of the *Anderson* radioed Captain Ernest McSorley of the *Fitzgerald* to discuss the threatening weather. It was during this conversation that the two captains agreed to take the longer, safer northern route.

McSorley was an experienced Great Lakes captain. His 44 years as a mariner began when he was an 18-year old deckhand working aboard ocean-going freighters. In 1950 he became the youngest Master on the Lakes.[5,6]

Throughout the exhaustive investigations into the sinking of the *Edmund Fitzgerald*, there was never any evidence that McSorley had been negligent, or responsible in any way for his vessel's loss.

McSorley and Cooper concluded their first communication by agreeing that a northeasterly course would be best. The gale warnings had just changed to storm warnings with projected northeast winds of 50 knots and the two masters wanted to be in the lee of the Canadian shore.

Both vessels made minor course alterations at 3 a.m. and the *Fitzgerald*, the faster of the two steamers, began to pull slightly ahead. The winds were now from the northeast at 42 knots.

For nearly six hours the two ships proceeded smoothly along similar courses. At 9:53 a.m. the *Anderson* headed due east, and an hour and 37 minutes later changed her heading to 125^0 T, proceeding southeastward, along the north shore. In effect, the *Anderson* was "cutting corners" and by doing so was able to keep up with the faster *Fitzgerald*. The *Fitzgerald* had travelled closer to the shore before heading south, according to officers in the pilothouse of the *Anderson*.

Both vessels had run into worsening weather conditions. Winds and seas continued to rise throughout the trip.

Shortly before noon, the *Anderson* changed course again, to 149^0 T. The weather had momentarily improved, with winds dropping to 30 knots. The waves were still running high — 10-12 feet.

At 12:52 p.m. the *Anderson* was 10.8 miles off Otterhead and altered course to 154^0 T. to clear Michipicoten Island's West End Light by two to two-and-a-half miles. The *Fitzgerald*, meanwhile, was about seven or eight miles ahead and somewhat to the east.

At 1:40 p.m. Captain Cooper of the *Anderson* radioed the *Fitzgerald's* McSorley to discuss an anticipated windshift. Cooper advised McSorley that he would be changing his course to the west before passing Michipicoten Island to be taking the rising seas from astern. McSorley said that he would continue on, since he had just cleared the island. He added, though, that his vessel was "rolling some."[7]

At 2:45 p.m. the *Anderson* changed course to 130^0T. to clear the Six Fathom Shoal area north of Caribou Island. The *Fitzgerald* was observed to be about 16 miles ahead. The northwest winds had swelled to a blistering 42 knots. Only an hour earlier they had been at five knots. A heavy snow began to fall and the pilothouse watch on *Anderson* lost sight of the *Fitzgerald*. The *Edmund Fitzgerald* was never seen again.

The northwest seas began to build with alarming speed. The Captain of the *Anderson* was deeply concerned about the Six Fathom Shoal area north of Caribou Island. He thought his ship would be cutting it close and made a course change to avoid the area. Although the *Fitzgerald* had disappeared from view, the *Anderson* had her on the radar screen as being 16 miles ahead and a "shade" to the right. Although no plot of the *Fitzgerald's* position was kept, watch officers on the *Anderson* observed her moving again to the right.

To those aboard the *Anderson* "watching" the *Fitzgerald* through the eyes of radar, she appeared to pass north and east of Caribou Island, and, as Captain Cooper later testified, closer to the Six Fathom Shoal than he wanted the *Anderson* to be.[8]

Meanwhile, the seas had been building and the winds stepping up their force. At 3:20 p.m., the *Anderson* recorded the winds to be howling at a steady 43 knots and the waves running up to 12 and 16 feet. Her deck was awash with heavy amounts of water.

Ten minutes later the *Anderson* received a call from the *Fitzgerald*, still invisible, somewhere in the storm. Captain McSorley reported that his ship had "a fence rail down, two vents lost or damaged and a list." Just how serious this damage was would become a future source for debate. It is important to note, though, that the *Fitzgerald* said she was slowing down so that the *Anderson* could catch up and keep track of her.

Captain Cooper then asked the *Fitzgerald* if she had her pumps going and was told, "Yes, both of them."[9] Radar on the *Anderson* now showed the *Fitzgerald* to be 17 miles ahead and a little to the right.

The *Anderson* made note of the damage aboard the *Fitzgerald* and agreed to keep an eye on her. However, no one in the *Anderson* pilothouse at the time of the last communication believed there was any reason to be concerned for the welfare of the *Fitzgerald.*

Only minutes later, the *Anderson* received an emergency broadcast from the Coast Guard: All ships on Lake Superior were directed to find safe anchorage. The locks at Sault Ste. Marie had been closed. The fierce November storm had finally received full notoriety.

Later, the Lock Master at the Soo was to state that his ane-mometer showed gusts over 90 mph and that water was sweeping regularly over the lock gates.[10] At one point vessels below the locks were reporting winds of 70 knots, gusting to 82 (96 mph!).[11] Even the Mackinac Bridge was forced to close down. Winds there had reached 85 mph.

Sometime between 4:00 and 4:30 p.m., the *Fitzgerald* had contacted the 490-foot Swedish saltwater vessel *Avafors* and asked if the Whitefish Point radio beacon and light were operating. The *Avafors'* pilot replied that she wasn't receiving the radio beacon and couldn't see the light. A little later the *Fitzgerald* learned from the Grand Marais Coast Guard that there had been a power failure and that neither the beacon nor the light were operational.[12]

About an hour after that call, the *Avafors'* pilot put in a call to the *Fitzgerald.* He spoke directly with Captain McSorley and told him that he had Whitefish Point's light in sight, but still wasn't receiving the beacon. At one point in this conversation, the *Avafors'* pilot heard McSorley shout to someone off-mike, "Don't allow nobody on deck!" He also thought he heard a vent being mentioned. When McSorley returned to his conversation with the *Avafors* he volunteered the information that the *Fitzgerald* "had a bad list, had lost both radars, and was taking heavy seas over the deck in one of the worst seas he had ever been in.[13]

At approximately 4:10 p.m. the *Fitzgerald* radioed the *Anderson.* Captain Cooper was temporarily away from the wheelhouse. The First Mate took the call. The *Fitzgerald* reported that both her radars were now out. She was in need of navigational help, and the *Anderson's* First Mate readily agreed to provide it.

At 4:52 p.m., the *Anderson* was abeam of and six miles off the tip of Caribou Island. On the radar the *Fitzgerald* was plotted at 14 to 15 miles ahead and a mile to the right. The wind was raging now. The *Anderson* logged them at 58 knots from the northwest, the highest winds thus far recorded during the voyage. Waves had swelled to 12 - 18 feet and a light snow continued to fall.

The *Fitzgerald* radioed again. It was just after 5 p.m. and the *Fitzgerald* wanted a position. The *Anderson* replied that she was 10.5 miles, 088° T. from Caribou Island light, reading the *Fitzgerald* to be 15 miles ahead.

The *Anderson's* First Mate then informed the *Fitzgerald* that Whitefish Point was 35 miles away.

At 6 p.m. the *Anderson* was 15 miles southeast of Caribou Island and was pulling out of its lee when waves as high as 25 feet came smashing across her deck. At 6:10 Captain Cooper went below and left the First Mate in charge of the wheelhouse. From what he could see on the radar screen, the First Mate thought the *Fitzgerald* was working her way to the left of the *Anderson*. He called the *Fitzgerald* to inquire about the apparent drift and the *Fitzgerald* reported maintaining a course of 141° T.

At 7:00 p.m. the *Anderson* again made radio contact and reported the *Fitzgerald's* position as 10 miles ahead and 15 miles off Crisp Point.

Ten minutes later the *Anderson* called again to issue a routine warning. There was another vessel approaching, nine miles ahead of the *Fitzgerald*.

The Coast Guard Report describes the exchange this way: "At 1910 (7:10 p.m.), the Mate called the *Fitzgerald* again and told them, 'There is a target 19 miles ahead of us, so the target is nine miles on ahead.' *Fitzgerald* asked, 'Well, am I going to clear?' and the Mate said, 'Yes, he is going to pass to the west of you.' *Fitzgerald* replied, 'Well, fine.' As the Mate started to sign off, he asked, 'Oh, by the way, how are you making out with your problem?' and *Fitzgerald* replied, 'We are holding our own.'" [14]

Those were the last words anyone ever heard from the *Edmund Fitzgerald.*

Captain Cooper returned to the pilothouse as this final conversation was being completed. At that time, the *Anderson* was 25 miles north-northwest of Whitefish Point. The officers observed the *Fitzgerald* on the radar to be nine miles ahead and a little over a mile to the east. This casual observation was to be the last time anyone on the *Anderson* was certain the *Fitzgerald* was on the radar screen.

By now the snow had stopped altogether and visibility in the storm-darkened evening improved. The wheelsman aboard the *Anderson* peered ahead and saw -- or thought he saw — two lights off the port bow. The lights were white and red, and the white one appeared to be forward of the red one. After studying them carefully, he decided the red light must be on the shore, and although he tried to point out the white light to the rest of the watch, no one else could see it.

While looking for the wheelsman's lights, the Mate saw some others. They were the lights of the *Nanfri, Benfri* and *Avafors,* three upbound saltwater vessels, about 17 miles ahead. The *Fitzgerald* was supposed to have been closer than those three ships, but her lights were nowhere to be seen. Captain Cooper thought the *Fitzgerald* might have suffered a power blackout and urged those on watch to study the horizon for a silhouette. Although the weather was clearing, they saw nothing.

Captain Cooper felt a deepening sense of alarm. The *Anderson* rapidly adjusted her radar and found three distinct targets. But they were the *Nanfri, Benfri* and *Avafors...*

Both the Captain and the Mate attempted to contact the *Fitzgerald* by radio. They reached no one. Thinking – and by now, hoping – that the radio might be out of order, the *Anderson* tried to contact the *William Clay Ford.* The *Ford,* anchored behind the shelter of Whitefish Point, received the *Anderson* loud and clear.

Cooper then called the Coast Guard at Sault Ste. Marie. He reached them on channel 16 and was instructed to switch to channel 12, normal procedure. When he did so, there was no follow-up. Cooper called the *Nanfri* to see if she had anything on her radar that might be the *Fitzgerald.* She didn't.

It was about 8:25 when the *Anderson* made successful contact with the Coast Guard in Sault Ste. Marie. Captain Cooper told them he'd lost track of the *Fitzgerald* on radar and that he was worried. According to Cooper, the Coast Guard was unimpressed, and told the *Anderson* to keep her eye out for a missing 16-foot boat in that area. Whether a 16-footer was missing was not Cooper's immediate concern. He believed there was a 729-foot boat missing, and 10 minutes after his previous call he radioed the Coast Guard again to make a stronger appeal: "I am very concerned with the welfare of the steamer *Edmund Fitzgerald.* He was right in front of us expecting a little difficulty. He was taking on a small amount of water and most of the upbound ships have passed him. I can see no lights as before, and I don't have him on radar. I just hope he didn't take a nose dive!"[15]

1. **MARINE CASUALTY REPORT,** SS EDMUND FITZGERALD; Sinking in Lake Superior on 10 November 1975 with Loss of Life, **U.S. COAST GUARD MARINE BOARD OF INVESTIGATION REPORT AND COMMANDANT'S ACTION,** Report No. USCG 16732/64216, Department of Transportation, Coast Guard.
2. Ibid.
3. Ibid.
4. Ibid.
5. **Marquette Mining Journal,** Marquette, Michigan, November 11, 1975.
6. **Toledo Blade,** Toledo, Ohio, November 11, 1975.
' 7. **MARINE CASUALTY REPORT,** SS EDMUND FITZGERALD; Sinking in Lake Superior on 10 November 1975 with Loss of Life, **U.S. COAST GUARD MARINE BOARD OF INVESTIGATION REPORT AND COMMANDANT'S ACTION,** Report No. USCG 16732/64216, Department of Transportation, Coast Guard.
8. Ibid.
9. Ibid.
10. **Sault Evening News,** Sault Ste. Marie, Michigan, November 11, 1975.
11. **The Toledo Blade,** Toledo, Ohio, November 13, 1975.
12. **Marquette Mining Journal,** Marquette, Michigan, November 11, 1975.
13. **MARINE CASUALTY REPORT,** SS EDMUND FITZGERALD; Sinking in Lake Superior on 10 November 1975 with Loss of Life, **U.S. COAST GUARD MARINE BOARD OF INVESTIGATION REPORT AND COMMANDANT'S ACTION,** Report No. USCG 16732/64216, Department of Transportation, Coast Guard.
14. Ibid.
15. Ibid.

THE SEARCH

The Coast Guard effort to locate the *Edmund Fitzgerald* began after the second radio call from Captain Cooper of the *Anderson.* That call was made at 8:25 p.m.

The Coast Guard immediately attempted to contact the missing ore carrier on VHF/FM and through the commercial radio station WLC at Rogers City, Michigan. Neither effort was successful, and it appeared that Cooper's original fears were being confirmed.

At 8:40 p.m. the Coast Guard Great Lakes Rescue and Coordination Center (RCC) at Cleveland, was notified. Just after 9 p.m., the *Anderson* took it upon herself to notify the Soo Coast Guard that the big ship was missing. This message was quickly relayed to the Cleveland RCC. At 9:15 p.m. the RCC directed the Coast Guard Air Station at Traverse City, Michigan to dispatch a search aircraft, and at 9:16 p.m. advised the Canadian Rescue Center at Trenton, Ontario, that an ore freighter named the *Edmund Fitzgerald* had vanished on Lake Superior.

The 110-foot Coast Guard cutter *Naugatuck* was resting in harbor at the Soo when a 9:25 p.m. call came in. Her orders were to begin an immediate search for the *Fitzgerald.*

The *Naugatuck* had been "down" for scheduled maintenance, but because of the storm, went into a temporary standby alert at 7:47 p.m. on November 10. Shortly after responding to the search orders, an oil line failed on the *Naugatuck* and she was forced to make hasty repairs. She wasn't underway again until 9:00 a.m. the following morning. It was 12:45 p.m. when the *Naugatuck* finally reached the search scene.

Even then, the *Naugatuck* was under heavy restrictions. Vessels in the *Naugatuck's* class are forbidden by regulation from operating in open water when the winds are in excess of

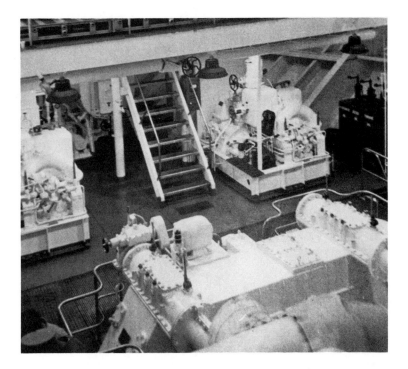

The *EDMUND FITZGERALD* — A Gallery

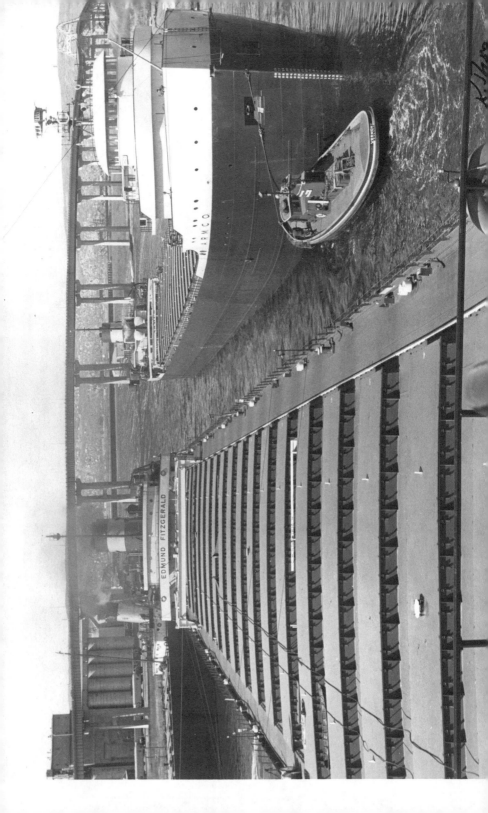

60 knots. Her initial instructions were to proceed no further than the entrance of Whitefish Bay and wait for better weather.

The *Woodrush*, a 180-foot buoy tender reinforced for ice breaking, was ordered to depart Duluth at 9:30 p.m. She was in a "Bravo Six Standby Status." That meant she was prepared to proceed in six hours. Strenuous efforts, however, enabled her to be under way at eight minutes past midnight. She reached the search area 24 hours later.

On the morning of November 11, one 40-foot Coast Guard Patrol left the Soo and searched until late afternoon. A 36-foot patrol boat at Grand Marais, Michigan and other 40-foot boats available at Duluth, Minnesota, Bayfield, Wisconsin and Marquette, Michigan, were not sent out because of the severe weather and long distances involved.

St. Ignace had 40-foot patrol boats and a 44-foot motor lifeboat which were also too far away to render assistance. The Coast Guard ice breaker *Mackinaw* was in Cheboygan, Michigan, undergoing repairs. The Coast Guard buoy tender *Sundew* was in Charlevoix, Michigan, also being repaired. Neither was able to assist in the search.

Aircraft from the Coast Guard also attempted to help. The first HU-16 fixed wing was launched at 10:06 p.m. and arrived at the search scene at 10:53. An HH-52 helicopter, equipped with a Night Sun (a 3.8 million candlepower Xenon arc searchlight), was launched at 10:23 p.m. It arrived at one o'clock the next morning. Additional Coast Guard aircraft and a Canadian C-130 fixed wing assisted. The search aircraft from Traverse City were supposed to be able to launch within 30 minutes, but another half hour was lost when night flares had to be loaded.

Commercial vessels were also getting into the act. The *Anderson* had turned around to look for the *Fitzgerald* at 9 p.m. By 2 a.m. she was back in the area of suspected loss. At 8:30 p.m. the Coast Guard had radioed for assistance from the American vessels *William Clay Ford*, *William R. Roesch*, *Benjamin F. Fairless* and the Canadian *Frontenac*,

Murray Bay, *Hilda Marjanne* and *Algosoo*. All of the ships contacted had been anchored in the shelter of Whitefish Bay. Of the seven ships, only the *Ford* and the *Hilda Marjanne* agreed to assist.

The Ford Company's 647-foot *William Clay Ford* was mastered by D.E. Erickson. It reached the area about the same time as the *Anderson* and searched until the following day. The *Hilda Marjanne* made a game effort to help but was driven back to the shelter of Whitefish Bay after 30 minutes. Conditions for a successful search were far from ideal.

The salties *Benfri*, *Nanfri*, and *Avafors*, who had all passed the area upbound, were asked to turn around and help look for the *Fitzgerald*. They all refused, claiming it was too dangerous in that kind of weather.

At 9:45 p.m. and again at 10 p.m. of November 10, the Coast Guard made urgent broadcasts, alerting all those who could hear that the *Fitzgerald* was missing and a search was in progress. Those broadcasts were to continue periodically until November 13 when the search was called off.

Other vessels responding to these later broadcasts and eventually assisting were Oglebay-Norton's steamers *Armco*, *Reserve* and *William R. Roesch*, U.S. Steel's *Roger Blough*, Inland Steel's *Wilfred Sykes*, Canada Steamship Lines' *Frontenac* and *Murray Bay* and the *Joan O. McKeller* of Scott Misner Steamships.

For three days the extensive but futile effort wore on. Coast Guard aircraft from Elizabeth City, North Carolina joined the already searching aircraft from Traverse City. C-130's from Canada and the Michigan Air National Guard helped out.

On November 13, at 10:12 p.m. the active search was suspended, but daily and weekly flights were maintained by the Traverse City Coast Guard until year's end.

The first clue to the location of the *Fitzgerald* was detected on November 14 by a Navy aircraft equipped with a magnetic anamoly detection unit (MAD). After searching approximately 100 square miles, the aircraft located an especially strong contact that was later identified as the *Fitzgerald*.

42

Prior to that discovery, the massive search effort had produced very little. Of the 29 men aboard the *Edmund Fitzgerald*, not a single survivor or body was found. Flotsam from the missing ore carrier was surprisingly slight.

Shortly after 8 a.m. on the 11th of November, a piece of one of the *Fitzgerald's* lifeboats was located by the *Anderson*. It was spotted nine miles east of the ship's eventual location. About an hour later another lifeboat was sighted four miles from the first. Eventually, the *William R. Roesch* discovered the No. 1 lifeboat off Coppermine Point. The *James D.* located the No. 2 boat in the same area.

A 16-foot section of the No. 1 lifeboat was found. It was so badly mangled it looked as if the missing portion had been bitten off by a mythological creature of enormous size and strength. The No. 2 lifeboat was still whole, but it too was badly mangled and buckled.

One inflatable life raft was discovered by the Canadian Provincial Police on the south shore of Coppermine Point. The other was recovered by the *Roger Blough* offshore.

Other items of flotsam included cork life preservers or pieces thereof, lifeboat oars, a sounding board, two propane tanks (used for galley fuel and stored on deck), life rings, a stool, a stepladder, boatcover, a searchlight and several pieces of scrapwood.

All tolled, it was a remarkably small amount of material recovered from the 729-foot carrier.

Several underwater searches were made to locate the hull of the *Fitzgerald*. The Coast Guard Research and Development Center conducted the first search from November 14 to 16. During that effort, a side scan sonar from the *Woodrush* located what was later identified positively as the wreckage of the *Edmund Fitzgerald*.

However, the original attempts to identify the wreckage failed; so a second search was made from November 22 through the 25th. Seaward, Inc., of Falls Church, Virginia used the *Woodrush* and again wind and sea conditions were severe. Sufficient data was gathered however, to positively identify the wreckage as the *Edmund Fitzgerald* this time.

A third side scan survey was conducted from May 12 to

May 16, again by Seaward, Inc., using the *Woodrush* as the search vessel. This survey was used to place the anchorage system for the photographic survey.

Between May 20 and May 28 the Naval Undersea Center's CURV (Cable-controlled Underwater Recovery Vehicle) system was used to conduct an underwater survey. Again the *Woodrush* was the "Mother ship." The CURV III was capable of making visual observations, recovering small objects and performing miscellaneous tasks to a depth of 7,000 feet. The CURV first made headlines in 1968 when it was used to salvage a nuclear warhead lost in 2,800 feet of water off the coast of Spain.[1]

The CURV III was a metal-framed vehicle measuring approximately six feet by six feet by 15 feet. It supported two horizontal propulsion motors, a vertical propulsion motor, a 35mm still camera, two black and white television cameras, various lights and a manipulable arm. An umbilical cord ran from the CURV unit to a surface control van on the deck of the *Woodrush*.

The CURV III logged 12 dives during the photo survey, totalling 56 hours. The survey took 43,255 feet of video tape and 895 color photographs. The official and final identification of the vessel was made at about 12:30 p.m. May 20 when the television cameras picked up the name "EDMUND FITZGERALD" upside down on her stern.

The CURV III unit and its operators were fully prepared to recover bodies during the search, but not one of the 29-man crew was located.

An independent research contractor reviewed the results of both the side scan surveys and the CURV III operations and prepared sketches of the wreckage.

The *Fitzgerald* is located about 17 miles northwest of Whitefish Point, just a bit north of the American boundary in Canadian waters. More specifically, it is 46° 59.9N, 85° 06.6W, in 530 feet of water.

The wreckage consists mainly of two major pieces — a bow and a stern section. The bow section is 276 feet long and resting rightside up. The stern section is 253 feet long and is upside down. The sections are about 170 feet apart. The distance between them is littered with torn metal. Both sections are deep in mud, and mud has covered much of the deck.

The exhaustive survey by the CURV III gathered a remarkable amount of photographs, video tape and information about the partially buried wreckage. Only one question remains unanswered — what happened to the *Edmund Fitzgerald?*

1.   **The Evening News,** Sault Ste. Marie, Michigan, May 21, 1976.

SHEARED RIVETS AND TORN METAL are evidence of the tremendous torque exerted when the *Fitzgerald* struck the bottom of Lake Superior. These rivets are estimated to be 1 inch in diameter.

Photo Courtesy of U. S. Coast Guard

THE COAST GUARD INVESTIGATION

NO SURVIVORS AND NO WITNESSES

The Coast Guard investigated extensively the details surrounding the loss of the *SS Edmund Fitzgerald*. The end result of months of exhaustive study of thousands of pages of transcript generated during the hearings was a statement of conclusions issued in late July 1977, by the Coast Guard Marine Board of Investigation. The Board was able to draw numerous conclusions, some of which remain open to speculation.

Those offering testimony included crewmen aboard other vessels in the vicinity of the *Fitzgerald* on the night she was lost, men who had served aboard her previously and company employees concerned with her general operation on the Lakes. Personnel representing the American Bureau of Shipping, the agency which had inspected and surveyed the *Fitzgerald* on October 31, Coast Guard personnel who had participated in the search effort, employees of the National Weather Service and men who had assisted with the loading of her final cargo at the Superior, Wisconsin ore dock were all questioned at length. Also considered was a great deal of information collected from various underwater photographic surveys conducted at the wreckage site.

The Board concluded from the lengthy testimony of officers aboard the *Anderson* that the actual course steered by the *Fitzgerald* could not be accurately reconstructed because no real "plot" of either the *Fitzgerald's* or the *Anderson's* course had been maintained. The *Anderson*, navigating by a series of radar readings and estimated bearing changes during the worst of the storm, had maintained no log of her positions which was of practical value in reconstructing the incident. The majority of testimony regarding navigational particulars hinged on the recollective capabilities of the officers aboard the *Anderson*. A conflict developed almost immediately from their testimony. The Board concluded only that if the *Anderson* had run all the courses to which her officers testified, her speed would have had to vary from 5 to 66 mph! The *Anderson's* engineering log indicated that she had maintained a steady 14.6 mph throughout the gale. It was obvious that some of the facts had been lost in the excitement of the *Anderson* pilothouse on November 10, 1975.

The Board also examined closely the difficulties reported to the *Anderson* by Captain McSorley aboard the *Fitzgerald*.

The Board stated that flooding which could have been expected through any two ballast tank or tunnel vent openings would not have been sufficient to have caused her loss. The list reported by the *Fitzgerald* — if it indeed had resulted from the previously mentioned source of flooding — would also not have been enough by itself to have caused her to sink in the opinion of the Investigating Board.

Captain McSorley had stated in radio communication with *Anderson* that he had (2) pumps going. As the *Fitzgerald* had six pumps available, the Board concluded that those aboard the steamer did not feel a serious situation was presented. Captain McSorley was aware of some flooding aboard his vessel and had been attempting to deal with it.

The "checking down" of the *Fitzgerald* to allow the *Anderson* to close up with her could well have been indication that Captain McSorley realized the difficulties with his ship were more serious than originally reported to the following *Anderson*.

The testimony heard and carefully scrutinized, the Marine Board concluded that there simply wasn't enough evidence to determine the "proximate cause of the loss of the *S.S. Edmund Fitzgerald...* "[1]

But the Board did determine that the "most probable"[2] cause was the flooding of the cargo hold, resulting in a gradual and almost imperceptable loss of buoyancy. The Board theorized that seas, sweeping the length of the open spar deck, had flooded into the holds through poorly sealed hatch covers and that the flooding of the holds had begun early in the gale. As the fury of the storm increased, so too did the amount of water accumulating below decks in the hold. The *Fitzgerald* slowly sank lower and lower in the water until the line between floating and sinking was passed. . . And she plunged.

The Board pointed to five separate factors which it felt had contributed to the loss of the *Fitzgerald*.

Her winter load line had been reduced 3'3¼" from that originally assigned in 1958. Reducing a load line actually means raising the load line markings on the side of a vessel so that more cargo can be loaded before she settles to that line. The "reduction" in load line means that more of the ship is permitted to run below the waterline, thus diminishing the vessel's freeboard — the amount of distance between the waterline and the deck. This significantly reduced the *Fitzgerald's* buoyancy and allowed more seas to board her in heavy weather, increasing the violence of the storm's assault on her and in turn, increasing the amount of water which would flood into the cargo hold through any poorly secured and/or poorly sealed hatches — or any other damaged area...

During the 1975 season of heavy and continuous iron ore trafficking, some of the hatch covers, coamings, gaskets and clamps aboard the *Fitzgerald* had become damaged. These damages usually occurred during cargo handling operations and there was no effective in-season program of maintenance for such equipment.. Such spar deck repair work was usually left until winter layup.[3] According to the Board, poor maintenance precluded the hatches from being watertight as required by Coast Guard Regulations.

A Coast Guard "ship-rider" program instituted in the fall of 1976 confirmed the Board's findings that the hatches indeed may not have been adequately secured. During the program, several vessels were discovered to have suffered various amounts of flooding resulting from non-watertight hatches and vent covers. [4]

It also appeared to the Board from studies of underwater photographs of the wreckage, that not all of the hatch clamps had been properly fastened, permitting even greater flooding to the cargo hold.

The Board felt that the massive flooding of the cargo hold

had probably gone undetected by the crew. There existed no method for sounding (determining the amount of water in) the hold and flooding could only have been determined to exist when the water level reached above the cargo of taconite pellets, a practical impossibility. . . The Board felt that if Captain McSorley had been aware of the massive flooding aboard the *Fitzgerald* that he would have been quick to take more positive steps to insure the safety of his vessel and crew.

The Board believes that Captain McSorley was unaware of his true situation when he reported to the *Anderson* that he had suffered topside damage and was experiencing a list. Erroneously attributing the list to the recently incurred topside damage, McSorley felt he had solved the immediate problem by engaging his pumps when, in reality, it was not the known topside damage which was responsible for the list. His pumps at that point were probably too late. He was taking on water and had already taken on too much. . .

The Board felt that the topside damage could have been caused when an unidentified floating object was taken aboard. Such an object could also have caused other undetected damage either above or below the waterline, but this entire point is purely speculative. With both radars inoperative, the *Fitzgerald* was sailing virtually blind through a snow squall. She could certainly have struck such an object without being aware of it. She made no report to the *Anderson* which would substantiate or disprove such a theory.

The breaking loose of an object stowed aboard the *Fitzgerald* could also have accounted for the reported topside damage, but the only objects on deck heavy enough to have caused such damage would have been a hatch cover, the spare propeller blade or the crane used to remove the hatch covers for loading and unloading. The Board felt that Captain McSorley would have reported any such incident immediately to the *Anderson*.

The damage could also have resulted from a grounding in the shoal waters north of Caribou Island or from the shuddering the *Fitzgerald* would have received from passing too near the shoal. Again, the damage could have been sustained either above or below the waterline. Since the *Fitzgerald* was reported, by the *Anderson*, to have passed near the shoal and because an accurate course plot could not be reconstructed, the Board concluded that a light grounding was possible. The shoal area in question had last been surveyed in 1919 and a resurvey conducted after the wreck of the *Edmund Fitzgerald* indicated a discrepancy in existing navigational charts.

The charts indicated a minimum of 30 feet of water over the shoal. With the *Fitzgerald* drawing 27 feet, she should have been able to safely pass over even in the shallowest areas under normal conditions. But when riding heavy waves and "pounding" in the seas, she would have drawn considerably more water.

Paul E. Trimble, Chairman of the Lake Carriers' Association, elaborated on the possibility in an article for the Detroit News in November, 1976. "I've been on ships pounding in a storm when you come down with a slam that makes you sure you have hit the bottom – and you know you've got a hundred feet of water under you. There is no way to be sure you haven't hit bottom. It is entirely conceivable – and I am personally convinced – that the *Fitz* was pounding and hit bottom on Caribou Shoals.

"Both *Fitzgerald* radars were out, it was snowing, visibility was poor and the winds were gusting to 80 knots. The master could not have known his position accurately. He may have thought he was clear of the shoals and his ship was pounding the sea when it actually hit bottom."

Divers did investigate the shoal area following the loss, looking for any sign of such a "pounding" – a recently smashed rock, scratches of paint. They found none. The lack of visible evidence, however, should not be construed as ruling out the grounding possibility.

The list reported by Captain McSorley might have resulted from a localized hull fracture or structural failure which caused a ballast tank (or tanks) to rupture and flood from outside the ship, but the photographic survey of the wreckage did not reveal any evidence which would support this theory.

50

The Board concluded that topside damage was "most likely" to have been caused by a collision with a floating object. They felt that this collision had probably occurred in the bow area, causing unseen and unreported damage which, together with the reported damage, had caused the *Fitzgerald* to be trimmed down by the bow. The downtrim at the bow caused water accumulated in the flooded cargo holds to move forward through the non-watertight cargo hold bulkheads, increasing the downtrim and the rate of flooding.

The result was that "the end was rapid and catastrophic... there was no time to warn the crew, to attempt to launch lifeboats or life rafts, to don life jackets or even make a radio call."

When Captain McSorley reported being in one of the worst seas he had ever seen to the pilot of an upbound Swedish freighter, he wasn't exaggerating. Through the day of November 10, his vessel had been mauled by increasingly severe weather. Every passing hour saw more and more water sweeping over the decks of the *Fitzgerald*, gaining entrance through the damaged topside and the aforementioned hatch cover areas.

As the *Fitzgerald* slowly lost freeboard and sank lower in the water, the effect of each sweeping wave was magnified. When the storm finally peaked, the *Fitzgerald* had lost so much buoyancy that the "bow pitched down and dove into a wall of water and the vessel was unable to recover. Within seconds, the cargo rushed forward, the bow plunged into the bottom of the lake, and the midship structure disintegrated, allowing the submerged stern section now emptied of cargo, to roll over and override the other structure, finally coming to rest atop the disintegrated middle portion of the ship."

The lifesaving gear aboard the *Fitzgerald* played no important role with respects to the loss of her crew. The plunge to the bottom had come so quickly and unexpectedly that there was no opportunity for its effective utilization. The lifeboats, judging from their damaged condition, had broken away from the vessel as she sank. The life rafts released from their float free racks and inflated as they were designed to...

51

The preceding pages are "fact." The information has been drawn from the Coast Guard Marine Board of Investigation Report, the Lake Carriers' Association Report (Statement), and various published news accounts concerning the loss of the S.S. Edmund Fitzgerald.   The opinions expressed were those of experts. I have purposely striven, thus far, to keep my opinions to myself — to not "editorialize."

This analysis of the Fitzgerald incident and the question-and-answer section which follows contain "my opinions," with the exception of those sources clearly acknowledged.

The reader should be clearly aware of this important distinction. What I am about to say here is the result of more than 10 years of shipwreck study on Lake Superior... and a careful examination of the details surrounding the loss of the Edmund Fitzgerald.

Although I have written extensively on Lake Superior shipwrecks, I had never intended to write an entire book on a single subject... But as more and more data came to light regarding this particular loss, it became apparent that there was more to the loss of the Fitzgerald than I had at first believed.

In common vernacular, the loss of the Edmund Fitzgerald has opened a "real can of worms." It is my sincere belief that the situation should be brought to the attention of the public... in its entirety.

Frederick Stonehouse

QUESTIONS AND ANSWERS

WHAT HAPPENED?

The chapter which follows contains portions of an interview I gave Steve Chandler of "South Shore" magazine, following the Coast Guard's release of its investigation findings. Editing has been done by Chandler and myself only for the sake of brevity. We allowed the answers to remain just as they were recorded. The interview was conducted on four different dates in October, 1977.

Q. *By writing a book about the shipwreck of the* Edmund Fitzgerald *are you not, to some degree, capitalizing on a tragic event?*

A. No, not now. Had I tried to write a book immediately after the loss of the ship, I'd have to say yes. But now that the Coast Guard's long investigation is complete, and all the evidence is available, I think a carefully reasoned examination of the ship's loss is possible.

Had you ever heard of the Fitzgerald *before she sank?*

No, I hadn't.

How did you first learn of the wreck?

I was sitting at home in Marquette (Michigan), that night. We'd been out diving and we'd come in and were drying out a little when a friend called and said, "We've got one missing off Whitefish!" At that point I tuned in the newscast and heard that yes, indeed, the *Edmund Fitzgerald* was "missing" off Whitefish Point. Then I just followed the story through.

Were you able to get any inside information from yor connections with the maritime community around Lake Superior?

No, but I don't think there was any inside information. I did get the inside track on the diving and survey that was done on Caribou Shoal, but my feeling was that there really wasn't any inside information available. Everybody was in the same boat of confusion.

From your background in shipwreck research, can you draw a parallel. . . is there another ship or ships that sank the same way the Fitzgerald *did?*

No. I would say no because we still don't know exactly why she sank. The two most popular — and plausible — theories are the faulty-hatch theory and the reef-striking theory. If the *Fitzgerald* sank because of faulty hatches, then we have forerunners in the *Henry B. Smith* and the *D.M. Clemson.* If we're talking about striking a reef, we limit our choices. I don't think there are any parallels on Lake Superior with the possible exception of the *Kamloops* which divers just located this summer. It's conceivable that the *Kamloops* struck a reef and sank.

NO EXPLANATION?

What about the idea put forth in the book, "The Great Lakes Triangle"? *The author said the* Fitzgerald *sank so quickly that there can* "be no worldly explanation" *for it.*

That's absolute nonsense.

Do you think there are reasonable explanations?

Sure. The Coast Guard's investigation and report made a good case for one. They thought hatch flooding could have done it. The Lake Carriers' Association presented another reasonable possibility — that she hit a shoal and holed herself without realizing it. There certainly are possibilities that can account for her loss.

At the time she went down, were you asked by the media to speculate on why the Fitzgerald *sank?*

The local newspaper and television station came by but there wasn't much I could tell them other than 'Yes, Whitefish Bay is the graveyard of Lake Superior, and yes, November is a nasty month on the Lake.'

In your other books about shipwrecks on the Lakes you've included some graphic passages about bodies discovered. . . and that sort of thing. Does writing about that aspect ever trouble you?

Shipwreck is not a pretty thing. It is very gruesome. One of the tendencies in writing about it is to make it appear to be romantic and it really isn't.

Do you ever think about the men who went down. . . on the Fitzgerald *for instance.*

Yes, I do, and it's a very terrifying thought! If we accept the theory that the bow of the *Fitzgerald* just dove into a wall of water, that would have destroyed any chance of using the pilothouse radio to call for help. But what of the poor men caught in the stern, or below decks, or in the engine room? They surely would have realized that death was staring them bang in the eye and that there was absolutely nothing they could do about it. How long does it take for an engine room or a sleeping compartment to flood? How many minutes does it actually take to drown under those circumstances? For that terrifying period of time those men certainly would have known what was happening and just how powerless they were to stop it.

When you're diving and exploring a wreck, does that thought ever occur to you. . . what were these men thinking in their final moments?

55

There are some instances. When crawling around on the *George M. Cox* off Isle Royale, you can see the engine and the boilers, and as you're crawling you realize that the impact of the collision with the reef knocked those things off their mounts! And the engines and boilers are huge! Or if you get on the *Algoma* where the plates. . . the steel and the iron. . . have been torn and twisted and shaped like they were paper. You get a real feeling for the power of the Lakes versus the ship. And to a degree, yes, you think of those final moments on the ship.

It's a much better feeling to be on a wreck like the *America*. She sank rather slowly, over a period of about 90 minutes, with no loss of life. But you find it so incongruous! You're down there, laying back, and here's the grand stairway going down. . . or else you're looking up from the salon deck, and the tile is still on the floor, and the tables and chairs are over in the corner. . . and it's oddly fascinating. You say to yourself, "What are the poor people doing today? Sitting home and watching 'Let's Make a Deal' on television!" And then you crawl over to another side of the wreck, and you start to dig in the silt a little bit, just to see what you can find, and the whole experience gives you a feeling of identification. . . you get a real sense of understanding the ship.

Have you thought of diving the Fitzgerald *wreck?*

No, she's far too deep. Commercial divers could do it. . . the technology is available. . . but what would be the point of them going down?

Might they not find out why she sank?

I don't think so. I just don't think you could come up with anything that would mean anything. It's not like an aircraft. It doesn't have a little black box that makes all the magic recordings.

Wouldn't there be a chance of finding a tear or an opening that could only have been caused by shoaling?

Yes, but the problem is the mud. By looking at the Coast Guard's sketches of how she's sitting on the bottom, you can see that those portions are so far covered with mud that a diver couldn't penetrate it. He wouldn't be able to see anything. And you're dealing with such a massive vessel! It would be like diving on the side of a skyscraper. Would you be able to identify something as being a hole even if you bumped into it? At that depth, even with lights, it would be very difficult.

But with a lot of time, and all the right equipment, couldn't a diver solve that orientation problem?

I'm sure he could solve it. . . yes. If he used all the equipment, and had all the time in the world. I still don't think he'd contribute anything to the total knowledge of the wreck. But that's not to say that in 20 years, when a quantum leap in technology allows everybody to jump down there and dive the *Fitzgerald* quite normally, that somebody won't find something. That's what happened with the *Andria Doria* — divers found that a vital bulkhead hatch had been left open.

Did you begin to form an opinion on the cause of the Fitzgerald's *loss from the day she went down?*

No. In fact, I tried to avoid becoming involved with it in the beginning. At that time we were so close to the incident, and there were so many wild theories flying around, that I just clipped everything out of the paper and kept a file on it with the idea that it would be something to go back on in two or three years and sort out what really happened.

I was living in Arizona when the Fitzgerald *went down, and we have very few shipwrecks out there. . .*

. . . very few, a lot of "wrecks" but very few shipwrecks. . .

. . .and the first real awareness I had, and most people I knew

had of the Fitzgerald *was from the song by Gordon Light-*
foot. What did you, as a shipwreck historian, feel about the
huge popularity of that song?

I though it was great! He did a reasonably accurate de-
scription of what happened. There's been some criticism of
his song, that he was wrong in some of his implications, but
I think the song was fantastic. However, some of the market-
ing techniques used. . . I'm not to pleased about.

Such as?

I saw a television promo for the album the song is part of,
and they played the song in the background, and while the
song was on, an animated cartoon appeared on the screen.
The cartoon depicted a body coming up and waving a grasp-
ing hand as the ship went down. It was the grossest thing I'd
seen in a long time. When you consider that the *Edmund
Fitzgerald* had gone down just a year ago, taking the lives of
29 men. . . well, that sort of promotion is just terrible.

WHY DID SHE SINK?

If you had to settle on one specific explanation for the sink-
ing of the Fitzgerald, *what would it be?*

I think I would agree with the Coast Guard's report.

The Lake Carriers' Association's president, Paul Trimble, de-
livered an awfully convincing rebuttal to the Coast Guard's
theory — that she took in water due to faulty hatches — and
suggested that shoaling was what took her down. Even after
reading the Lake Carriers' letter, are you still leaning toward
the Coast Guard's explanation?

Yes. The Coast Guard did the most thorough job of investigating. I feel that, unlike the Lake Carriers, the Coast
Guard had no vested interest in the outcome of their investigation.

Don't the Lake Carriers have a strong case for suggesting she struck Six Fathom Shoal?

Yes, they do. And really, what I'm probably doing is leaning 70% one way and 30% the other, because I just don't know.

Did the wreckage that was picked up offer any clues to the sinking of the Fitzgerald?

No. It was everything that you would have expected if the vessel had just been swept under. . . life rings, life jackets, some oil. . . floating debris that would have come loose from the deck.

Does discovered wreckage ever shed light on the cause of a vessel's sinking?

Usually not. In the case of the *Clemson*, though, the discovery of hatch covers on the beach indicated that she'd probably been lost due to storm action and that the vessel sank from flooding. The discovery of furniture from the deckhouse or pilothouse might suggest that the seas had worked the vessel over before she sank. But that would apply to older vessels only. . . vessels that had wooden deck houses and not steel ones. In most instances, very little can be learned from the discovery of wreckage.

What about the Fitzgerald's *mutilated lifeboat?*

Other than the metal lifeboat found after the *John Owen* loss in 1919, which was also badly battered, I don't remember any lifeboat being found in a similar condition. But we have to remember that very few vessels have sunk with steel lifeboats. In the past the lifeboats were almost all wooden. The damage to the *Fitzgerald's* lifeboat was probably caused by its going down still secured to the ship. Because of its buoyancy, she would have broken loose from the stern as the *Fitzgerald* sank and struck the vessel on the way up.

Does that tell us anything about the loss?

No.

What is your opinion of the recently-advanced "three sisters"
theory. . . that three abnormally large waves overwhelmed
the Fitzgerald?

There's no evidence for it. That theory suggests that the
Fitzgerald was running with the northwest seas, three un-
usually large waves swept aboard from astern and met on her
forward half. The combined weight of the waves then forced
the *Fitzgerald* to bow under and literally submarine. The
newspaper article I read which first advanced the theory contained quite a few factual errors. The writer was inaccurate
in describing the dimensions of the vessel, the depth of the
water and the track of the last voyage. When so many key
facts are in error, it makes it hard to support the article's
conclusions.

But, errors aside, could not the theory itself be valid?

I don't think so. Remember that the *Fitzgerald* was not the
only ship in the area that night. The 767-foot *Arthur M.
Anderson* was only eight miles or just behind the *Fitzgerald,*
experiencing identical sea conditions. Relatively speaking,
the *Anderson* was just as heavily-laden as the *Fitzgerald,* and
would also have been vulnerable to the "three sisters." The
647-foot *William Clay Ford* participated in the search for the
missing *Fitzgerald.* Being in ballast, she took more stress than
a loaded vessel. She also should have been easy prey to the
"three sisters" phenomenon. The Coast Guard report had
already theorized that a larger than normal wave forced the
Fitzgerald's bow down and contributed to her sinking.
Nevertheless, that suggestion has no connection to the "three
sisters" theory. I've got to conclude that the "three sisters"
theory is wholly unrealistic and just another one of many
theories that will probably be advanced annually on the an-
niversary of the *Fitzgerald's* sinking.

DID SHE BREAK IN TWO?

Is there any chance that due to pure stress and a structural weakness, the Edmund Fitzgerald *simply broke in two?*

Actually, there's historical precedent for that. Some authorities thought the *Morrell* and *Bradley* sank due to structural failure. Another steel carrier, the *Western Reserve*, broke due to stress. That, though, was prior to the turn of the century. (August 30, 1892, off Deer Park, Lake Superior.) But the reason for that was the type of steel they were using. It wasn't capable of taking the type of stress combined with cold. She simply broke and sank. However, neither the Lake Carriers nor the Coast Guard in their reports thought there was any real possibility that the *Fitzgerald* broke simply due to stress.

Do you agree?

Yes, completely. There's no evidence for it.

Did the ship receive any modifications — such as lengthening which would have left her vulnerable to structural fatigue?

The *Fitzgerald* was never modified to increase her length. Although she received several strengthening modifications during her lifetime, none were considered very serious, or even odd. So, in this instance, no. Modification could not have had anything to do with her going down.

What about unrepaired damage from previous voyages? Is there a chance the Fitzgerald *was in such a state of disrepair that she took on too much water somewhere and sunk?*

The damages that were logged on the hatches prior to the vessel leaving could not have caused the loss of a ship. They could have resulted in seeping or leaking, but certainly not massive flooding. The problem may have been damages that were not reported, which could have been bad gasket seals, perhaps, on the hatches, that would have looked fine, looked very routine and not even have been logged as a deficiency. Something like that might have contributed to the flooding of the vessel.

Do you think the captain of the Fitzgerald *might have known, near the end, that his ship might be facing a catastrophe?*

I don't think anybody on the *Fitzgerald* had any knowledge of anything being amiss. Somebody might have developed some kind of sixth sense which might have told them that *something just doesn't feel right.* Or else the captain might have had the thought, "my God, I've been pumping and pumping and we're not making any headway." But to have had any real idea of what was happening? No, absolutely not.

What would he have been able to do if he had known?

Assuming he had knowledge of the specific nature of the damages to his vessel, step one would have been to notify the Coast Guard. To let them know exactly what was happening. Then he would have undoubtedly asked the *Anderson* and other nearby vessels to close up with him immediately to provide some possible chance of a rescue.

Would that have been a very reasonable chance?

Sure. Had the *Anderson* closed right up to the *Fitzgerald* the chance would have been very reasonable.

Isn't that kind of ship-to-ship rescue kind of "touch and go" in a storm like the one on November 10?

It's very touch and go, very chancy, but it's a heck of a lot better than nothing. And it's what I think the *Fitzgerald* would have opted for. From the *Anderson's* behavior in the gale, which I thought was quite praiseworthy, we can assume she would have done everything possible to have assisted the *Fitzgerald.* It's also not unlikely that some of the other vessels in the area would have closed in on her for the same purpose. I would be surprised, however, if the effort was successful beyond 50% of the crew.

Do you think the vessel-to-vessel rescue efforts would have saved half the crew — rather than say, the Coast Guard? [1]

If anybody was to be saved, it probably would have been through the efforts of the *Anderson*. I don't think the Coast Guard, in that storm, would have been able to utilize her helicopters at all. No surface craft could have gotten there on time.

LAST WORDS

It seems to me, in light of what finally happened, that the radio-communication dialogue between the captains of the Fitzgerald *and the* Anderson *seemed remarkably subdued. In that fierce storm, and with acknowledged damage to the ship, why didn't they act a little more frantic. . . or at least concerned?*

It's very common that on the Lakes the captains say very little to each other. They don't give out a lot of information over the air. If a captain is in trouble and sinking, certainly he'll say so. But if he just has 'problems,' (and a problem could be anything from a spilled cup of coffee to taking tremendous amounts of water), and he doesn't feel his vessel is in any real danger, he's not going to tell anybody.

Why not?

He's not that anxious to spread his problems out over the airwaves. A radio on a ship is a very public thing, anybody can listen in on it.

And admitting to having problems might make him look less like a captain?

71

Perhaps that's part of it. These guys do have a lot of pride. They've been out there — many of them — for 40 years or more. They just don't give out a lot of information over the radio. They're in a business. They do that job for 260 odd days a year. . . or more. . . and it's as routine to them as driving a car is to us.

In those final hours in the storm, when the captain of the Fitzgerald *was in contact with the* Anderson, *do you think the captain knew where he was, or do you think he was pretty much winging it as far as finding a course for himself?*

I think he knew. . . I think he knew fairly well where he was. Of course with his radars out of commission, and in that blowing gale, there was bound to be a little uncertainty. I think, however, he knew basically what his course was.

Well, how much leeway did he have with that uncertainty? How safe was it to be even a little uncertain?

Let me explain it this way. I feel that he knew he was close to Caribou Island. He was certainly aware of the charted shoal north of Caribou Island. He had no reason to expect that the charts were in error. It was revealed in testimony that the *Fitzgerald* was closer to the shoal than the *Anderson* skipper would have wanted to be. . . but even had he known that, I still don't think he'd have thought he was in any danger.

Did any of the ships that were in the area of the Fitzgerald *that night run into any serious trouble?*

Nothing that would have even approached causing the loss of a vessel. When the Coast Guard put out a call for assistance to look for the missing *Fitzgerald*, however, only one ship responded. That was the *William Clay Ford*. The others all felt it was too dangerous, and they either stayed where they were, or turned around and looked for shelter. The upbound "salties" said they would keep their eyes open while proceeding on track, but they would not turn back to make a search, although the evidence on that is a little contradictory.

THE STORM

At what point during the storm do you think the ships out on the Lake knew this was a once-in-a-lifetime storm?

After it was over. There were a lot of confused readings that day. They closed the Mackinac Bridge, and there were 90 mile an hour winds below the Soo. But they were only reporting 62-63 knots from the *Anderson* in the area that the *Fitzgerald* went down. But then the weather bureau came back and made the claim that the storm was really not *that* severe. So you have a problem in these conditions really getting an accurate weather data picture. It's very difficult.

Do you think the captain and crew aboard the Anderson *demonstrated enough concern for the safety of the* Fitzgerald?

Absolutely. Those people deserve to be commended. In fact, they were the only ones who demonstrated any real concern for the *Fitzgerald*. If the *Anderson* had not reported that they thought the *Fitzgerald* was gone, the Coast Guard still might not have missed her to this day. . . Well, perhaps that's extreme. Logically, they would have missed her when she didn't get to where she was going. But that would have been the only way, unless somebody at the Soo was smart enough to figure out that she didn't lock through. And they really don't keep a very tight list of those things. . . you know, it's not like a train. With a train, if one comes ahead of it, and one comes behind it, and you're missing someone in the middle, you know something's wrong. But on the Lake it doesn't work that way.

Looking back. . . was that pumping the Fitzgerald *admitted to be doing any cause for alarm?*

Not at the time. It didn't seem to be that much of a problem. They'd lost a couple of vents, they were taking on a certain amount of water, and they had the pumps on. They had a bit of a list, and they were in a 70 mile an hour gale, but that's really not so uncommon! Then they lost their radar, but still there was no cause for alarm.

Wasn't there anything that might have indicated that things were not under control?

Yes, there was. There was an overheard radio communication from the *Fitzgerald*. . . I think it was a pilot on one of the upbound ships that overheard the *Fitzgerald* captain say "Don't allow nobody on deck!" and something unintelligible about vents. That was perhaps the most revealing remark.

Doesn't it sound to you like he was hiding his problems? Shouldn't he have been more forthcoming?

Well. . . I just don't know. That overheard remark doesn't necessarily indicate a severe condition. When those big boats are loaded and moving in any kind of heavy seaway, it's very common to have waves right across the spar deck. That's why communication tunnels have been built into so many of those ships. The *Fitzgerald* had them. The tunnels run from stem to stern all the way under the decks. The *Fitzgerald* had one on either side. In a storm with heavy seas a crew can move through the tunnels in relative safety.

If we accept that the captain didn't know he was in any danger due to damage to the vessel, isn't it possible that there was topside damage that he knew about but didn't see cause to mention?

Yes, and that's the possibility the Coast Guard presents. That she did have topside damage that they were reacting to. . . that they thought it was under control, when, in reality, they had much more damage than they were aware of, and that this is what was causing all the flooding.

FRUSTRATING MYSTERIES

It all seems so mysterious. Isn't there anything the Coast Guard could have done after the loss to eliminate some of these frustrating mysteries?

Of course. Consider this: The *Fitzgerald* went down taking 29 men with her. Before they really got serious about investigating the loss it was next spring! That's when they brought out the CURV (Cable-controlled Underwater Recovery Vehicle) and started taking pictures of it. That's the same CURV unit they used to recover the A-bombs lost off the coast of Spain. If it had been an A-bomb that had been dropped in Superior instead of the *Fitzgerald* you know they'd have been there *the next day* with that CURV unit.

When should the Coast Guard have gone out?

If the lives of those 29 men, and the lives of the men in vessels still out on the Lake had really been the Coast Guard's primary concern, they would have been out there right away — that fall — to find out what happened. Not the following spring when the ship's been settling in the mud for four months.

Is the mud that bad?

It was a major problem in surveying the ship. The mud covers an awful lot of that ship right now.

How did they justify waiting so long?

Their justification was the weather. And it's true, weather conditions are better in the spring.

Was it impossible for them to investigate the Fitzgerald *that fall?*

Of course not. They were out there three times to make sonar surveys to get a fix on her location.

Do you think the video tapes and photographs eventually taken of the Fitzgerald are a sufficient exploration of the remains of the ship?

Considering the time lapse and the mud there was nothing better they could have obtained.

If they'd gone down immediately following the loss, what more could they have found?

There may have been a better chance of examining that section of the wreck which could have touched on Caribou Shoal. They could have, perhaps, done a better examination of some of the hatch clamps. They may have learned a lot more than they eventually did.

How much of the Coast Guard sketches of the Fitzgerald as she sits underwater do you believe is speculation?

I don't think any of the sketches are speculation. They certainly took enough photographs. I think they put a good mosaic together and came up with accurate sketches. However, the part you're just dying to see is the part that's under the mud. And you can't see that.

From those sketches, the ship looks like she broke right in half.

Yes, but how much of that would have been done as she sounded? If she'd rammed her bow into the bottom, the pure impact plus the shifting cargo would have torn the *Fitzgerald* asunder.

SIX FATHOM SHOAL

The Lake Carriers say that the "only thing" that could have happened to the Fitzgerald was striking Six Fathom Shoal. Do you agree?

Of course not. There are many different things that could

have happened. Nobody from that wreck survived, and the wreckage has only been marginally surveyed. To say that shoaling is the "only thing" that could have happened is really stretching their point. It is a likely thing, and it is a logical thing, but it isn't the only thing.

What did the Coast Guard think of the shoaling possibility?

They examined the possibility. They were not able to determine, they felt, whether the *Fitzgerald* did cross over the Caribou or Six Fathom Shoals. No track of her course was kept. The *Anderson* didn't keep a record either of her location relative to the *Fitzgerald*. On that basis they didn't think it likely that she hit Caribou Shoal.

Wait a minute. Just because there isn't a written record of hitting the shoal, they rule it out?

In the examination of the officers of the *Anderson* they ran into a real problem in that nobody really knew where the *Anderson* was either. I think they made a comment in the report that if the *Anderson* had been everywhere each of her officers said she was, she would have been moving, at various times, between 5 and 66 miles per hour. What they're saying is that because they don't know where the *Fitzgerald* really was, they can't be sure she hit a shoal.

That sounds like pretty weak grounds for dismissing a possibility of cause.

It is. It's a very weak argument. The Lake Carriers, in their letter of rebuttal, did seize on a very weak point in the Coast Guard report.

You've already alluded to the tremendous pride the Lake captains have. Is there a chance that the captain of the Fitzgerald *knew that he'd grazed a shoal near Caribou but was unwilling to mention it?*

I don't think that has even a grain of possibility. As closed-

77

mouthed as those masters may be, they certainly are not fools. These men are charged with real responsibility — not only to their vessels, but to the lives of their crew. They're well aware of the immense damage that can be done to a vessel by just touching a shoal. I'm sure the captain of the *Fitzgerald* would have gotten right on that radio and let people know.

It seems to me that the Coast Guard would have given more attention to the shoaling theory since it would have made them look much better. If the ship had hit a shoal, there's no reason for safety and inspection methods to come under fire.

That's right. That's part of the reason why the Coast Guard report is so convincing. If you're looking for an ulterior motive, the shoal theory would have been just fantastic for the Coast Guard. If they had concluded that the *Fitzgerald* had hit a shoal, especially since it was in Canadian waters that turned out to be poorly charted, then the Coast Guard would be absolved from any blame.

So you're still leaning toward the findings of the Coast Guard report?

Yes. The Coast Guard considered all the factors. . . they took volumes and volumes of testimony over many months of investigation. We have to conclude that they did a thorough job.

HYDROGRAPHIC SURVEY

The last hydrographic survey of Caribou Shoal had been taken back in 1919. Isn't that unusual?

That case is only a little bit extreme. Soundings that were taken in the 20's and 30's are still being used today. Consider the case of Superior Shoal. Superior Shoal sits out in the middle of the Lake about 18 miles off the steamer track from the Soo to Thunder Bay, and it rises from a depth of 720 feet up to 20 feet. In some areas it's even shallower. It's about 2,500 yards in diameter, but it wasn't discovered until 1930! They never knew it was there until a Lake survey ship accidentally blundered across it while making routine depth surveys. But that type of discovery on the Lake is common because of Superior's underwater topography. Lakes like Michigan and Huron have primarily sand bottom and sand shores. On Superior, sand is the exception rather than the rule. The Whitefish Bay area is an exception. Almost everything from Marquette west is rock.

The survey taken after the Fitzgerald *sank revealed an extension of Caribou Shoal which had been uncharted. Do you think, on the whole, that Superior has been properly surveyed?*

Before the *Fitzgerald* sank I certainly would have assumed it was surveyed well enough. On the basis of the discovery of the extension of Caribou Shoal, the evidence would have to indicate that it probably isn't.

Isn't hitting a shoal something that could take a ship down immediately?

Yes, it very well could. It would depend on the way she hit the shoal and the depth of the water and the damage that was done. If she hit and did the damage that the Lake Carriers suspect. . . such as ripping out several ballast tanks. . . see, their premise is that when she hit she didn't rip her cargo hold out, rather she hit and ripped several of her ballast tanks. This would have resulted in massive flooding. . . of the ballast tanks. The *Fitzgerald* skipper said that he was pumping following the passing of the shoal. But the pumps he had going were ballast tank pumps, and because he'd reported that there were missing ballast vents on the spar deck that were lost, washed off or damaged, it was assumed that he was pumping water coming through those tank vents. In reality, he could have thought that too. But he might have been pumping all this time green water coming through the bottom, which he never could have kept up with. . .

. . .*Green water?*

That's solid water. In a gale a ship takes spray over the decks, but to take "green water" over the decks means that a whole wave is coming across. . . and it's not just foam.

SAFETY RECOMMENDATIONS

The Lake Carriers recommended that vessels be required to carry a "hull-monitoring" system. What are they talking about?

It would work much the way a cardiac patient in an intensive care unit has his vital signs monitored. There is a central read-out from which the ship's captain can monitor the "vital signs" of the vessel in times of stress. They install a monitoring unit along critical hull areas and the various stress points read out in the pilothouse.

Could that have saved the Fitzgerald?

It's hard to be sure. If the *Fitzgerald* had been equipped with such a system, and she had shoaled or hit something, it would have read out immediately as overt stress in that area.

Why would the Lake Carriers, who are already reacting strongly against what they consider to be "expensive" Coast Guard recommendations, submit even more recommendations?

I think, after reading the Lake Carriers' recommendations, that it's strictly a show. An example is the hull-monitoring system you ask about. If they had really wanted it on their vessels they'd have put them on by now. They also recommend an all-weather survival capsule and survival suits as a new safety possibility, and damn it, those things have been in use for over 20 years!

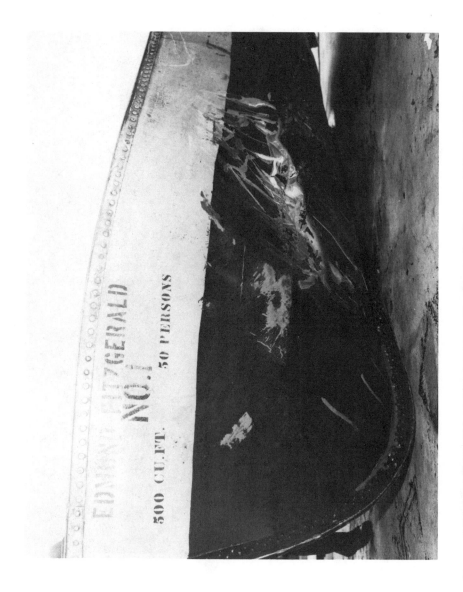

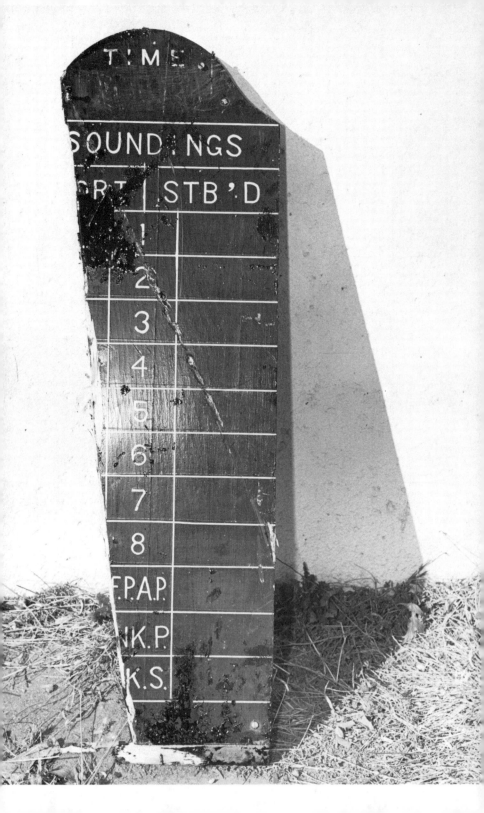

Do you think survival capsules would work on Great Lakes vessels?

Yes, I do. They've been used with great success on the offshore oil rigs. If a rig is in danger, they get into the capsule, seal it up and eject themselves into the sea. It's equipped with radios, food, survival gear, locating beacons. . . when the gale abates, and rescue is possible, they come over and pick the people out of the capsule. It's very practical, and wouldn't be that expensive.

Do you think the Lake Carriers would have brought it up if it was expensive?

I think the Lake Carriers are trying to make a case for themselves about how safety-conscious they are and have been. But of course they're still looking at that balance sheet of safety commensurate with cost. They're saying, in essence, "We're going to be as safe as we can be for our dollar."

That survival capsule idea sounds so simple. It seems like it makes a realistic concept of the lifeboat idea.

Well, I wouldn't eliminate the open lifeboat entirely. A lifeboat is a handy thing to have. You may for some reason just have to get out and get down to the side of the vessel. Or you might be in port, loading, and just want to do a little checking. That's when it's convenient to put the lifeboat or work skiff out. You can use it, come back, and haul it aboard. But you're right, it's really no longer a viable life-saving tool. In years past of course, they carried lifeboats, and a yawl boat was used as a general skiff boat. It worked fine.

WAS THERE EQUIPMENT FAILURE?

Was the radar operational aboard the Fitzgerald *when she sailed?*

The radars were not reported to be not operating. So the assumption is made that they were functioning.

Would they necessarily have been reported as not operational?

There is no reason to assume that they would not have been. Before the *Fitzgerald* left Superior, Wisconsin, she had made a request for a radio repairman to be standing by when she arrived at her destination to work on one of her radios. But this was not even a primary radio. If she made that request, she'd certainly have made a request if radar assistance had been required. The *Fitzgerald* made no mention of radar trouble throughout the trip until the very end when she asked the *Anderson* to keep track of her. We have to assume that everything was in working order up to that time.

What sort of sounding gear was carried aboard the Fitzgerald? *Was it sufficient?*

When I read about it, I was appalled! The *Fitzgerald* had no electrical sounding gear, no depth gauge, no fathometer, nothing. Or nearly nothing... She had a hand lead, which is a page right out of Mark Twain. It's a piece of lead with a line on it. You run to the bow of the vessel, throw it out, and count the number of knots in the line. It's absurd, incredible. . . it makes absolutely no sense.

Is it unusual?

I don't know. . . but it's astounding! To my way of thinking, electronic sounding gear would have been one of the cheapest pieces of gear a ship could carry. $200 - $300 would put electronic sounding equipment aboard. If you think about the trade they're in, going into docks, through channels, where they're working with controlled depths, if they do stay within the guidelines of the buoys and channel markers, they would never have to know exactly the depth of the water they're in. The water is maintained at a minimum controlling depth safe for navigation. But for that rare circumstance, such as the *Fitzgerald* went through in the storm, sounding gear is vital and necessary.

What sort of apparatus are you talking about that would do the job for 200?

A simple transducer that's mounted on the hull with a reading indicator in the pilothouse. It's essentially the same item you buy in a sporting goods store for $59 to put on your rowboat to go fishing with. They call it a fishfinder... A fathometer is only a little more sensitive. They range in price from $60 to several thousand dollar recording sonar rings, but I think anything in between would be of great benefit to any commercial vessel.

How might the Fitzgerald *have used that equipment on her last trip?*

If the *Fitzgerald* were coming up on Caribou Island and she wasn't sure just how far off shore she was, her radar was out of commission and she knew she was running near a shoal. . . Damn! The pilothouse crew could flip on that fathometer and say, "Wow, we're in 36 feet of water, we're in a world of hurt, let's get out of here!" And even if they wouldn't have gotten out they could have passed the information on to the *Anderson.* But without that simple piece of equipment, they would never have known, perhaps never knew. . . it might have given those on board a clue.

INCREASED CARGO

What do you think of the practice of changing the loadline regulations on a ship so that it can carry more cargo?

I am really amazed that they can build a vessel under one set of criteria and then at some later point change those criteria and still retain the safety of the original design.

Would the Edmund Fitzgerald *have been safer with a lower loadline if, in other words, she hadn't had to ride so deep in the water?*

91

Certainly. From the time the *Fitzgerald* was launched to the time she sank they had continually increased her limits. This meant she carried more cargo with each alteration and she sat deeper in the water. If she is lower in the water during a gale, it means more water over the decks which, of course, increases the chances of flooding. If they hadn't been so enthusiastic in loading those ships, they'd be a little safer.

How do you think that attitude compares with the attitude of the auto industry or the airlines?

I think the airlines' safety concern is the highest. There, everyone works toward it. . .

. . . but they have a vested interest in safety on airlines don't they? If people are afraid to fly, business is down, whereas on an ore carrier. . .

. . .That's right. There is really no vested public interest in safety on the Great Lakes. The same thing is true for ocean-going trade. There's no vested public interest in whether an ocean freighter sinks. . .unless it causes an oil spill.

Do you think that lack of public interest is one of the reasons why the Coast Guard is under so little pressure to improve its standards?

I think so. Whether they realize it or not I think it's a major contributing factor. If they were running a Great Lakes passenger service — where there would be two or three hundred people on board one of those boats regularly, then the Coast Guard presence on the Lakes would have to be much larger than what it is now. I hope it would, anyway.

Do you think, then, that the enormous publicity surrounding the loss of the Fitzgerald *will act in a positive way. . . that it might bring more pressure to bear to make the ships safer out on the Lakes?*

I'm afraid I'm very cynical about that. The Great Lakes ore carrier is the most commercially efficient vessel in the shipping trade today. But it's nothing but a motorized barge! It's the unsafest commercial vessel afloat. It has virtually no watertight integrity. Theoretically, a one-inch puncture in the cargo hold will sink it.

What, then, do you mean by efficient?

Dollars per ton per mile. . . of effective cargo space. . . or however you measure it.

Do you foresee any changes in basic design?

Well. . . They've been building them this way since 1900. It's tough to overturn 75 years of designing tradition. Many of the 1906 and 1907 vessels are still in trade today. And, really, the design of the new ones, other than being larger, is even worse than the old. For example, the older vessels such as the *Fitzgerald* , and she was a youngster as I've mentioned, are designed with ballast tanks which are located on the underside of the vessel and along the sides. They control the depth of the vessel, and, to a degree, its sea-keeping ability. They also serve the fine function of being partial collision bulkheads. So if you puncture a ballast tank, the tank floods but the vessel doesn't. Of course, if too many of these tanks are punctured in the wrong circumstances, you'd lose the vessel anyway. At least you have some margin. But with some of the new vessels you don't even have tank configuration, so, theoretically, that one-inch hole will sink her.

SAFETY ON THE LAKES

Is there a case to be made for improving the weather forecasting on the Lakes?

I don't think it would have made any difference in the *Fitzgerald's* case. She plowed right on, regardless. Unless she'd had a fair and clear warning of a truly severe gale coming... And even then, I'm not sure that she'd have delayed her departure from Wisconsin. These vessels work a very tight schedule. They're supposedly built to punch their way through heavy weather and despite storm forecasts, the *Edmund Fitzgerald*, I believe, would have continued.

So you don't think improved weather forecasting would help matters?

Improved weather forecasting would be a tremendous advantage if we could get it. More reporting stations, and more personnel. I would like to see it purely for my own use as a diver. But I couldn't say that the forecasting on the Great Lakes is really in an inefficient state. It's pretty good. Should it be improved? Sure.

Does it seem to you that we have entered an age of complacency? That because it had been so long since a major ship was lost. . . that maybe we had come to think that it just couldn't happen anymore?

I think that's very true. It's a complacency on all of our parts. The sinking of the *Fitzgerald* was a great shock to everyone. Even the Coast Guard, in their report, indicates that there's a very lackadaisical attitude on the part of vessel owners, masters, crews. They recognize that this problem exists.

Will they correct it?

No, I don't think it will ever be corrected. As long as there are 20 years between major wrecks. . . where is the real stimulus to work on your life saving capabilities?

Are the men on the ships today less capable of saving themselves than the sailors of the past were?

That's part of the problem. Fifty and a hundred years ago there were *sailors* out there on the Great Lakes. They were real seamen. Today that's not true. The men of today, for the most part, are just not sailors. Even the Lake Carriers'

Association made the concession that the seamanship of today is not what it had been in the past.

Is that because the ships are safer. . . because there's less need to be a good sailor?

I don't feel it's that. It's really because the whole nature of the trade has changed. For what they're doing, in many instances, crewmen aboard the ore carriers might as well be working in a factory. It's just not a sailing profession anymore.

And those crewmen are going out on the Lakes knowing that their safety equipment is little more than a joke?

Yes, they are. The Great Lakes mariners are very fatalistic. The time for survival in water for a man is measured in minutes. If you're out in the water you're going to freeze to death. You're not going to make it. One of the pilots of one of the ships testified at the *Fitzgerald* hearings that if he knew his ship was going under, he'd just climb into his bunk and pull his blanket over his head and that would be it. He wouldn't even think of the life-saving equipment. He'd just accept it. And, really, that's not an uncommon feeling.

So you don't believe that any kind of survival equipment at all could have saved the men of the Edmund Fitzgerald?

No. The evidence is that the wreck was so sudden and so catastrophic that no known survival gear could have saved the crew.

1. There have been numerous instances of successful rescue efforts by commercial freighters on Lake Superior. On May 11, 1953, the efforts of the JOSEPH H. THOMPSON, D.M. CLEMSON, WILFRED SYKES and HOCHELAGA responded to the radio distress call of the rapidly sinking HENRY STEINBRENNER, managing to save 14 of her 31 man crew. On May 1, 1940, the grain-laden Canadian freighter ARLINGTON foundered 12 miles east of Superior Shoal when a furious gale opened her hatches. 16 of her 17 man crew successfully abandoned her in a lifeboat and were picked up by the freighter COLLINGWOOD. The lone casualty was the captain who refused to leave his vessel. He was part owner, it was his first trip in command and the first trip of the season for the ARLINGTON.

LIFE JACKETS RECOVERED FROM THE *FITZGERALD* WRECKAGE AREA, are displayed in this Coast Guard photograph. They were stored above deck and floated free when the carrier sank.　　　　　Photo courtesy of U. S. Coast Guard

AN EPILOGUE

A CONSPIRACY OF INEPTITUDE

The loss of the *Edmund Fitzgerald* revealed a glaring and tragic deficiency — namely, the lack of a viable Coast Guard rescue capability on Lake Superior.

When the *Fitzgerald* was lost, all that the Coast Guard could muster was a buoy tender at Duluth, Minnesota (320 miles distant), a 40-foot utility boat and a harbor tug (both in a "repair status" at the Soo), a collection of small motor lifeboats at Marquette and Grand Marais, Michigan and Bayfield, Wisconsin, and of course, the grab bag of the Coast Guard Auxiliary. All in all, it's a fine group for locating lost sport fishermen in the middle of summer, but a force absolutely inadequate to the real Coast Guard mission — rescue at sea! With the exception of the buoy tender *Woodrush*, stationed at Duluth, none of the craft mentioned above could have survived the storm which claimed the *Fitzgerald*, let alone rescue anyone!

In the terrible sea conditions which prevailed on the night of November 10, 1975, even the *Woodrush* would have been severely "tested."

To more fully understand this remarkable — deplorable situation, an examination of the Coast Guard on the Great Lakes is in order...

The Coast Guard's presence on the Great Lakes dates from 1876 when the United States Life-Saving Service began operations. Several Life-Saving Stations were in operation on Lake Superior in 1877. More followed in succeeding years.

Within a short time, the Life Saving Service had become legendary. Many contemporary journalists referred to its members as "Heroes of the Surf", "Storm Warriors"...[1]

The U.S. Coast Guard was formed when the old Revenue Cutter Service and the Life-Saving Service were merged in 1915. The personnel, equipment and missions of each were combined and incorporated into the new Coast Guard.

As the Coast Guard had simply absorbed the legendary Life-Saving Service *en masse*, that organization's renowned tradition of seamanship and professionalism carried over to the fledgling Coast Guard for a time. I personally believe that today's Great Lakes Coast Guard is still living on that legendary reputation.

This is not to imply in any fashion that the individual Coast Guardsman of today is any less courageous than his Life-Saving forebearers, but a lack of adequate equipment, sufficient training and proper command philosophy has hamstrung him to a state of comparative inefficiency in this time of super cargo ships.

During fiscal 1975, the Coast Guard on the Great Lakes, (Ninth District), and the St. Lawrence responded to more than 8,000 calls for assistance. Of this number, 278 were in Lake Superior and 352 in the area served by Coast Guard Group Sault Ste. Marie. The Soo Group's area of responsibility includes extreme northern Lake Michigan, the Straits of Mackinac, the St. Mary's River and northern Lake Huron. In 1975, the Coast Guard on Lake Superior claimed to have saved 19 lives and $92,000 worth of property.

During this period the Coast Guard's heaviest workload was generated in western Lake Erie, Lake St. Clair and connecting waterways in the Detroit vicinity. This area accounted for 53% of the Coast Guard effort. All of Lake Superior and the additional area served by Group Soo accounted for only 6% of total Great Lakes' missions.[2] This figure is somewhat misleading because it does not take into full account the disproportionately larger number of privately owned pleasure craft in use on the lower lakes.

The Coast Guard Great Lakes' fleet is hardly impressive. The Coast Guard vessels are small... And they are old.

Vice Admiral Paul E. Trimble (USCG Ret.), President of the Lake Carriers' Association, best described the situation when he said, "None of these vessels were designed specifically for Fourth Seacoast duties. In fact, no vessel has been built for Great Lakes service since the World War II era. The duties, the operating environment and the available technology have changed considerable since then. As might be expected, the Coast Guard vessel fleet has grown exceedingly tired in the intervening years and it is increasingly difficult to supply with parts support for, and assure the traditional Coast Guard reliability."[3]

To handle an ever-increasing workload, the Coast Guard had (in 1975), 3 air stations and 46 coast stations, 9 of which were operated on a "seasonal only" basis. Lake Superior and the Group Soo area had only 9 stations, 3 of these auxiliary-manned, and no air stations.

The entire Ninth District Coast Guard had only five 180-foot buoy tenders (*Woodrush Class*), five 110-foot harbor tugs (*Naugatuck Class*), 2 major icebreakers and one 82-foot patrol boat. Hardly an impressive fleet!

Of 22 44-foot motor lifeboats (fine medium rescue craft), none were stationed in the Lake Superior — Group Soo area.[4]

As of July 1976, the Coast Guard was planning to 'eventually' replace the 110-foot harbor tugs, admitting that they were subject to "severe operating limitations in heavy weather." The tugs are very sensitive in winds over 40-45 knots. They become unstable and unsafe. When the weather is cold, they ice up badly. ". . . these characteristics severely impede their usefulness in the vicious sea and wind conditions that often occur on the Great Lakes."[5]

With these limitations one wonders why such vessels were ever assigned to a rescue mission on the Great Lakes in the first place!

One new 140-footer is scheduled to be stationed at the Soo, but by Coast Guard admission, it will only provide "reasonably heavy weather capability."[6]

The 140-footer will have a speed of 18 knots, a considerable improvement over the *Naugatuck's* top speed of 9. Four of the new tugs are being built at a Tacoma, Washington shipyard at a total cost of $18.7 million. The new tugs were designed as part of an experimental program to extend the Great Lakes shipping season the year around.[7]

Generally speaking, Coast Guard rescue response times are also most unimpressive for Lake Superior. The following chart, taken from the previously referenced hearings, is indicative —

CRAFT	Munising	Portage 1 Keweenaw Bay	Portage 2 Upper Entry	Isle Royale
Surface	1h 51 min.	2h 50 min	5h 18min	5h 32 min
Fixed Wing	1h	1h 18 min	1h 29 min	1h 41 min
Helicopter	1h 53 min	2h 31 min	1h 54 min	3h 18 min

To fully understand the significance of this chart, a little extrapolation is necessary. If for instance, a unit is already underway or in the immediate area, the response time can be significantly shortened. But the reverse could just as easily be true. The unit could be elsewhere.

Should the unit be committed or if the weather is bad, response times could be much longer. . . The important thing for the reader to bear in mind here is this chart's implications as they relate to the Coast Guard's *mission* of saving life at sea.

It seems entirely unsatisfactory that portions of Lake Superior are more than 5½ hours from surface Coast Guard assistance and over 3 hours from helicopter aid — providing that the weather is good! [8]

EPILOGUE 2

In the case of the *Fitzgerald* disaster, the Coast Guard aircraft dispatched to the scene from Traverse City, Michigan, came equipped primarily as search tools, not as rescue vehicles. They are especially helpless, from a rescue standpoint, in the wind and sea conditions which prevailed. The first aircraft on the scene, a fixed-wing HU-16, was ordered out from Traverse City, Michigan at 9:15 p.m., but didn't arrive in the Whitefish Bay area until 10:53 p.m. The first helicopter didn't arrive until 1 a.m. In view of the fact that Lake Superior aircraft resources are based at Traverse City, the time lag is understandable. . . That does not make it desirable!

Mr. E.L. Slaughter, Vice President of the International Longshoremans' Association, in testimony at the previously mentioned hearings, said he felt facilities were required which would allow a 15-20 minute response time. There certainly is room for improvement in this important area.

Coast Guard aircraft aren't even the best available. The HH-52s (helicopters) are aging and the Coast Guard only has "hopes" of replacing them "someday" with new short range recovery aircraft. As of July, 1976, the Coast Guard had no money available and wasn't in a buying posture.

The overall rescue shortcomings on Lake Superior are well illustrated by the following "What If" situation—

Suppose, for example, that several of the crewmen from the *S.S. Edmund Fitzgerald* did, through some miracle, survive the sinking of their ship and that they somehow reached one of the lifeboats which broke free and bobbed to the surface. Half drowned, freezing to death, showered by wave after wave of icy water, they cling there for dear life, waiting for the rest of the miracle — rescue.

Against all hope they begin to burn signal flares which remained with the damaged lifeboat. Another miracle... A searching Coast Guard aircraft spots the signal flares and makes the proper report.

Now what?
The men lie dying in the bottom of the lifeboat. Sinking into shock, the effects of hypothermia begin to manifest themselves. The men are slowly dying from exposure, freezing to death. They hang on desperately. Each huge wave

threatens to sweep them back into the lake.

The aircraft circles above, unable to land in the wild sea. Even a helicopter rescue attempt would be "dicy" at best, but there is no helicopter...

The Coast Guard's best answer would be to vector in the nearest surface rescue craft. . . But there are no Coast Guard surface rescue craft capable of reaching the men in the lifeboat.

So "What If?"

The answer is simple.

The men die!

This morbid hypothetical situation can be projected a step further by adding the supposition that Captain McSorley aboard the *Fitzgerald* realizes his ship is sinking and immediately issues a call for assistance.

What Coast Guard equipment would have been available to rescue his crew in the near-hurricane conditions which existed?

The answer is again a simple one... Terrifyingly simple for anyone who earns a livelihood aboard a Great Lakes cargo vessel!

NONE! ZERO! ZIP!

Although other commercial vessels were in the general area, they were unequipped and their crews untrained for rescue. They cannot, could not have been, relied upon for assistance. The rescue mission is the responsibility of the Coast Guard!

The Coast Guard is much like a fire department. You hope that they will never be needed, but when they are, they better be superbly trained and equipped for their task because there will be no second chance. The principles of cost accounting only make sense to those penny pinching congressmen and budget-minded admirals who can afford that luxury in the comfort of a warm, dry, safe office. To those in trouble cost accounting is sheer lunacy!

It's high time we considered the balance sheet more carefully... Took a look at the bottom line, as it were, to see if the dollar expenditure is equal to the task at hand: Saving Lives.

The Coast Guard claims 19 lives saved in 1975, but how many lives were lost that should have, could have been saved if the Coast Guard had been adequately equipped to carry out its task. Twenty-nine lives were lost in a single incident in November 1975, which is not to say that the Coast Guard could have saved the life of one *Fitzgerald* crewman in view of the circumstances, but what if there had been more personnel to conduct inspections, to enforce lifeboat drills, and what if the circumstances had been different?

The Army, Navy and the Air Force prepare themselves in every conceivable fashion to do something which everyone hopes they will never have to do again: fight a war.

To that end however, men are trained, equipment is purchased and forces are deployed. If none of the training, the equipment or the forces are ever used, their mission has still been successful. And if there is need, they are prepared.

The Coast Guard should operate on that same type of philosophy. That a station does not save a single life in 20 years is unimportant. That it saves one life makes it worthwhile and a station should be in a state of preparedness which assures that it will be able to save that one life when the time comes. That a small percentage of rescues are staged in a particular area is insufficient grounds for not fully covering that area with the best possible rescue protection that can be mustered.

That the Coast Guard is not the efficient life saving force it should be is regrettable and the situation should be changed.

With respects to the loss of the *Fitzgerald* the Coast Guard is certainly not deserving of all the flak it has received. The Lake carriers themselves deserve a sizeable share of the responsibility if responsibility can be placed.

Mr. John Bluitt, Port Agent, Seafarers International Union, River, Rouge, Michigan, in testimony before the previously cited committee, called the ore carriers ". . . little more than one large shell — they have no watertight compartments and the self-unloaders have one continuous conveyor belt underneath the cargo holds. They are completely hollow with no watertight compartments. We believe that these vessels should no longer be allowed to be built in this manner, posing an enormous risk to the lives of the crewmembers."

In those hearings, Daniel L. Smith, Marine Engineers Beneficial Association — Associated Maritime Officers, AFL-CIO, Toledo, Ohio, testified, "The frightening thing about the loss of the *Fitzgerald* and her crew is the great speed with which the vessel went under. The men aboard apparently had no time to don life jackets or launch lifeboats. We know the *Fitzgerald* was taking on water; the cargo holds must have flooded almost immediately because the *Fitzgerald*, no exception to the Great Lakes' rule — was not equipped with watertight bulkheads between cargo compartments. The ship was lost within minutes after she was stricken.

"Contrast this with the story of the *SS Maumee*, an ocean-going tanker that struck an iceberg near the South Pole recently. The collision tore a hole in the ship's bow large enough to drive a truck through, but the *Maumee* was able to travel halfway around the world to a repair yard, without difficulty, because she was fitted with watertight bulkheads.

"It is amazing that a stricken ocean tanker, her bow nearly torn off by collision damage, can travel halfway around the world for repairs while one of our very best Great Lakes freighters, taking on water from a still undetermined source, could not make it 55 miles to the safety of Whitefish Point.

"It is my opinion that watertight bulkheads, required on all ocean-going ships, have never been required on Great Lakes vessels because most of the people in Washington who write the laws are doing so with the mistaken impression that the Great Lakes are really little more than a bunch of 'knee-deep ponds'."

The Coast Guard Underwater Survey of the *Fitzgerald*

Photos and Sketches Courtesy of the U. S. Coast Guard

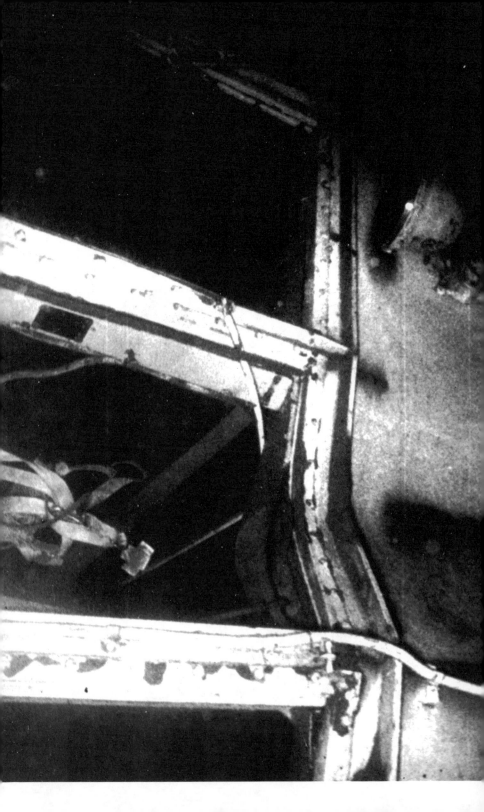

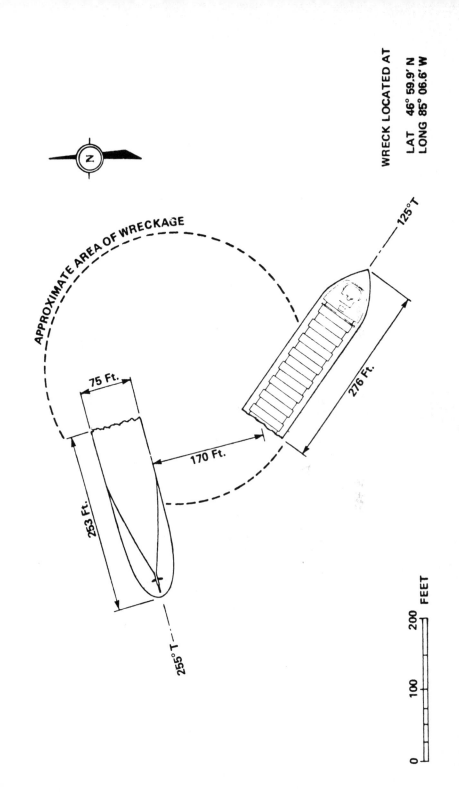

APPROXIMATE AREA OF WRECKAGE

75 Ft.

170 Ft.

253 Ft.

255° T

276 Ft.

125° T

WRECK LOCATED AT

LAT 46° 59.9' N
LONG 85° 06.6' W

0   100   200   FEET

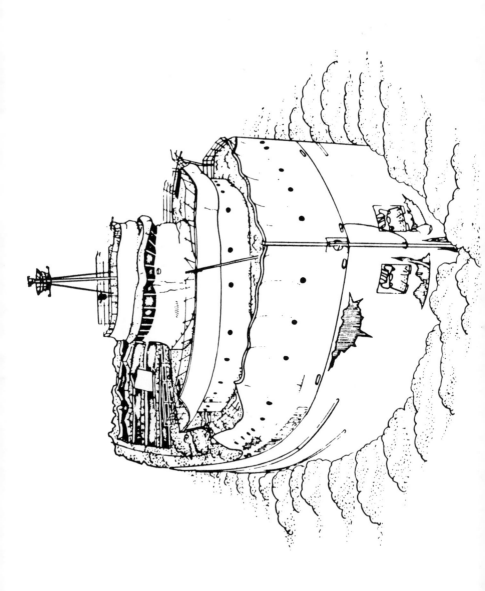

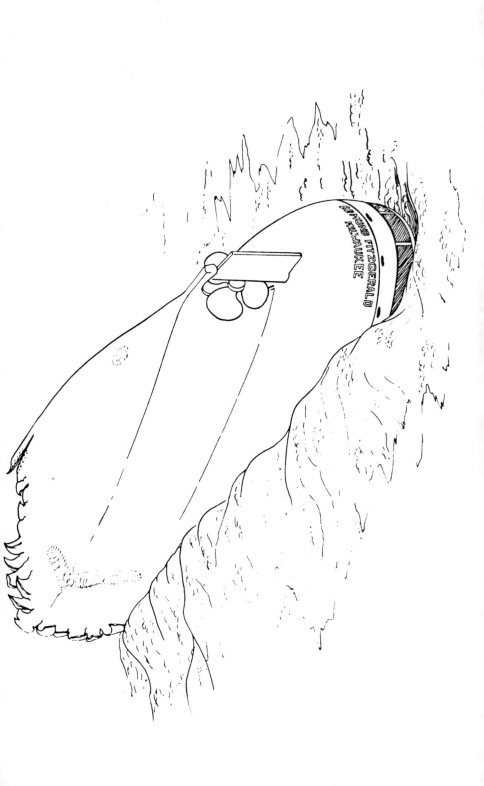

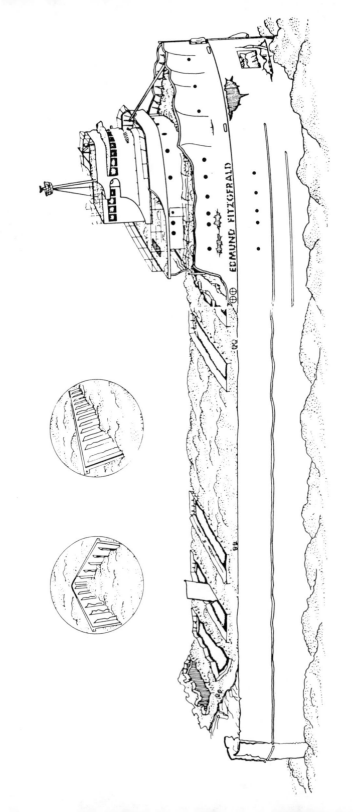

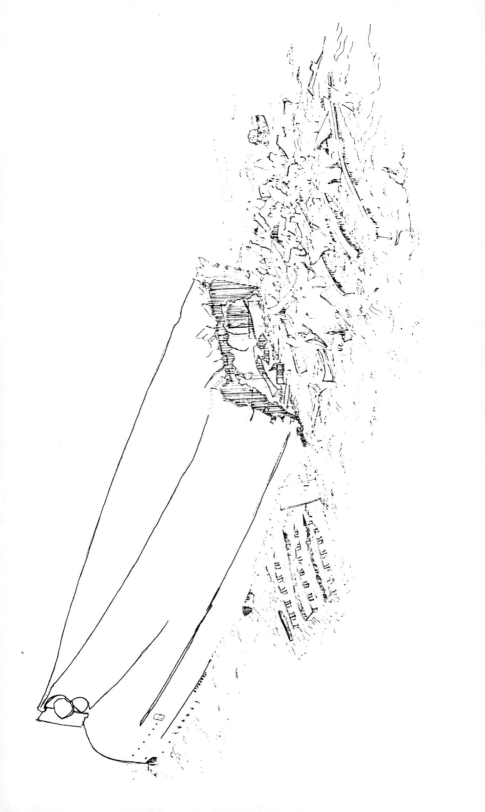

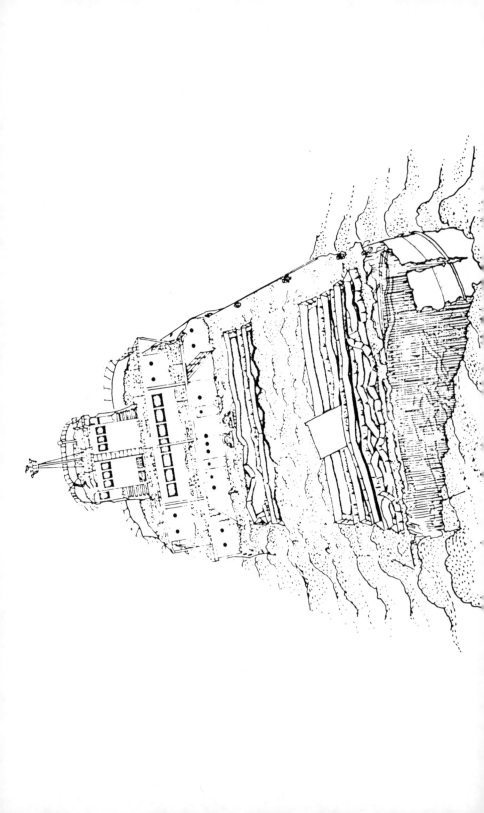

I would sometime like to have the opportunity to address those lawmakers personally — as Fred Stonehouse, diver, shipwreck historian – on my "turf" and in my fashion. They could perhaps be jammed aboard a Coast Guard 44-foot utility boat in the Soo and treated to an enjoyable excursion ride to a point just beyond Whitefish Bay where we could speak without interruption. I could be waiting to meet them in an open lifeboat:

"Ladies and Gentlemen, welcome to God's country. You are probably wondering why I have gathered all of you here today. Well, it's to draw your attention and that of the American public to the presence of a 729-foot ship lying broken in the mud nearly 600 feet beneath where we stand... in this 'knee-deep pond' we call Lake Superior. I would like you to appreciate the fact that this was a giant ship. If we could stand her on end, she would still tower up some 200 feet above the water. It was huge and this water is deep!

"That ship and the 29 men who went down with her shouldn't be there and I was hoping that some of you would have some suggestions which might preclude the necessity for us having to keep meeting like this to discuss other things that shouldn't be...

"And now, if you'll excuse me, I have some pressing Affairs of Fishing to attend to. If you will all step to the bow of the boat, I will have someone pull the plug beneath your feet. I will radio the Coast Guard for assistance while you are deliberating your decision and offering any suggestions which might come to mind.

"Yes, The Lifeboat recognizes the Senator from the great state of .. . .

"Yes, Sir. I understand that it's cold. About 34 degrees, but just keep treading water, Sir. I'm certain help will be here in a few minutes."

Watertight bulkheads should be required on all Great Lakes vessels. Great Lakes shippers maintain that such bulkheads would increase loading and unloading times, cut into valuable cargo space, and curtail the efficiency of their operations. But it's time we decided whether men or machinery are more important, whether cargo payloads are more important than human life.

I would hope that the answer would be obvious. I fear that it is not, that the question will simply be ignored as though never asked.

But if shipping must be slowed down somewhat to insure the safety of those aboard the Great Lakes fleet, then so be it. It is time to stop saving money for the sake of increasing profits at the expense of the vessel crewmen. We must insist that no more corners be cut which will further endanger the lives of those men who move the ships...[9]

And what does it amount to? What have been the results of all the months of hearings, the volumes of testimony, the attractively packaged Coast Guard Marine Board Report, the sharp looking statement of the Lake Carriers' Association, complete with two-color letterhead and employing the best debating techniques ever committed to print...

I believe it all has boiled down to pointing out a massive *Conspiracy of Ineptitude* generated by apathy at every level of the political, economic, military, bureaucratic humdrum that is born of affluence and a dwindling appraisal of the worth of the average human being.

Consider the circumstances as they pertain to the loss of the *Edmund Fitzgerald* on the night of November 10, 1975.

First consider the shortcomings of the Coast Guard:

The Whitefish Point radio beacon was inoperative. Both the Whitefish Point light and the radio beacon had a three-year history of failure. The signal and monitoring system were carried (in 1975) in the same ground line which provided telephone service to the Whitefish Point area north of Paradise, Michigan. People can perhaps live quite nicely without reliable telephone service, but when reliable service was needed most, when the captain of a huge lake carrier was looking to that radio beacon for navigational assistance which might have enabled him to save his ship, it had failed. There is no excusable reason that can justify such repeated failures when the cause of those failures is recognized.

It is not beyond the realm of possibility that Captain McSorley did use his Radio Direction Finder in a forlorn attempt to receive the Whitefish Point beacon. With her radars out and unable to quickly pinpoint his vessel's position because the beacon was out, the *Fitzgerald* could have plowed over the dreaded Caribou Shoal. The Marine Board of Investigation glossed over this prospect in my opinion.

The Coast Guard on Lake Superior was in a low state of heavy weather rescue preparedness. Surface craft were undergoing repair or were too small or too far away to have been of assistance. There is a 60-40 probability that a November search and rescue effort on the Great Lakes would have to be conducted during hours of darkness. That even a half-hour delay occurred while a search plane loaded flares for a night search is ludicrous. When needed most, the vessels which were available were either not capable of offering assistance or were not equipped for the performance of their primary task... A branch of the Department of Transportation, except in time of war, the Coast Guard exhibited a lack of expertise which it has not displayed in time of war... A lack of funding and the absence of "combat" readiness born of peacetime complacency was manifested.

There was a poor response to the initial *Anderson* radio communication to Group Soo. The switch to channel 12 failed and valuable time was lost before Captain Cooper was able to re-establish radio contact with the Coast Guard and emphatically announce his belief that the *Fitzgerald* was lost. This delay was inexcusable.

The Coast Guard waited until spring 1976, before undertaking photographic surveys of the *Fitzgerald* wreckage. This seems an inordinately long period. There was apparently no greater sense of urgency in determining the possible cause of her loss than there had been for accurately assessing the situation and taking immediate, appropriate action on the night she was lost.

An inaccurate, but trusted, chart of the Caribou Shoal area by the Canadian Hydrographic Service didn't help matters on the windswept lake in November 1975. We have the technology to update existing navigational aides so that these discoveries do not arise to haunt us again.

The Lake Carriers are also subject to shortcomings and should not be allowed to mask their partial responsibility for the loss of the *Edmund Fitzgerald* behind the smokescreen argument centered around whether the *Fitzgerald* did or did not sink from shoaling. . .

The *Fitzgerald* carried no system for monitoring possible cargo hold flooding and could not have successfully pumped the hold, (assuming it had been discovered or even suspected), when the hold was filled with cargo.

There were no watertight bulkheads between cargo holds.

Insufficient lifeboat drills, half the required number, had been conducted. That the crew of the *Fitzgerald* had no opportunity to use the lifeboats is immaterial. Training in their use was neglected.

Hatch cover maintenance was being delayed as was custom until winter layup. An inspection conducted only 10 days prior to the loss of the *Fitzgerald* revealed these deficiencies and still she was allowed to sail in what is historically the month of storms on Lake Superior.

Although it was widely known by the Lake Carriers, vessel crews and the Coast Guard, that conventional lifeboats could not be successfully launched during a storm, no real effort was made by any of these groups to lobby for the adoption of a life capsule system similar to that used on offshore oil rigs. Bringing up the necessity for such survival gear at the hearings conducted to investigate the loss of a vessel and her entire crew, when such equipment is available and proven, but has not been placed aboard commercial vessels because it as yet wasn't required is the weakest of all arguments.

On a similar note, exposure/survival suits, in use since World War II, were recommended by both the Coast Guard and the Lake Carriers, but again there had been no effort to see that they were adopted prior to the issuance of a "regulation".

A near total lack of initiative relative to precautionary survival/safety upgrading on Lake vessels on the part of owners, operators and the Coast Guard is to be deplored. Regulations should not have to be updated on a wreck-to-wreck basis... It should be possible, indeed desirable, to institute those measures which will insure that there are witnesses around to explain what happened should another great ship go down.

When all the points are tallied, a draw results with respects to arguments concerning cause, responsibility and initiative for designing safe vessels, instituting better inspection techniques, providing more adequate survival gear... But it's too late to make any difference in the case of the *Edmund Fitzgerald*.

The tally would indicate an inconclusive draw — a stand off — and it points to a conspiracy of ineptitude born of those causes outlined at the beginning of this segment. That there are not more wrecks of the *Fitzgerald* nature is almost remarkable!

In the two years since the *Fitzgerald* disaster, what additional resources has the Coast Guard deployed to Lake Superior? Pitifully little...

Grand Marais, Michigan received a 44-foot motor lifeboat, (MLB) in the place of an antiquated 36-footer. [10]

117

Marquette, Michigan received a 44-foot MLB to replace its 40-foot work boat.

Bayfield, Wisconsin received a 41-footer in place of its 40-footer.

The North Superior Station, (Grand Marais, Minnesota), was reactivated.

A policy has been adopted which would eliminate the scheduling of planned repair of major Coast Guard vessels during the historically bad weather months of November and April. [11]

How can we insure against future *Fitzgerald-type* disasters? What steps can be instituted to creat a viable Coast Guard rescue capability on Lake Superior?

For openers, the Coast Guard recommendations put forth in the *Fitzgerald* report should be adopted. Lake carriers should be required to have watertight bulkheads separating cargo areas. This would require expensive retrofitting as pointed out by the Lake Carriers' Association, but it is a sensible recommendation... In future, ship designers and builders will consider designing Lake carriers after a fashion resembling ships rather than "motorized super-barges."

The Coast Guard must look to the establishment of an air facility at some centrally located point from which it can serve Lake Superior. [12] In the interim, the stationing of aircraft, both fixed-wing and helicopters, should begin at K.I. Sawyer Air Force Base near Gwinn, Michigan in Marquette County.

A major ice breaker should be stationed at a central point, either Marquette or Munising. If docking facilities are not available, they should be built. A major ice breaker would be capable of handling rough weather, providing all-weather rescue capabilities and could perform normal ice breaking duties.

Each existing Coast Guard Station on Lake Superior

should be equipped with at least one 44-foot MLB. This would include the Portage Ship Canal Station on the Keweenaw Peninsula.

A final comment is warranted concerning the new 1000-foot class lake freighters and the potential which they offer for a new era of super shipwreck exposes.

The new 1000-foot class lake freighter is an example of technology and the bulk carrier concept gone wild. The new 1000-foot *Belle River* for instance, recently carried a cargo of nearly 60,000 tons - - - more than 1½ times the combined weight of the *Edmund Fitzgeral* and her cargo on that last trip! Just maneuvering these 1000-foot behemoths is a problem and their presence on the Lakes is going to create some problems.

It is my personal belief that the 1000-foot (and many of the smaller 800 plus footers), pose an entirely new set of safety problems. For one thing, they are so large that they can't get into many ports or protected areas, forcing them to remain "outside" in heavy weather instead of seeking shelter.

The new carriers are far too large to use the Keweenaw Waterway (The Portage Lake Ship Canal) and must make the long exposed run around the Keweenaw Peninsula. A similar problem is encountered by many of the larger carriers under the 1000-foot mark. The 858-foot *Roger Blough* is an example.

But in the Great Lakes' trade, bigger vessels mean cheaper transportation costs and the ore carriers continue to grow and grow, limited only by the size of the locking facilities at Sault Ste. Marie. And even this obstacle does not pose a finite limit. The Lake shippers are already agitating for either an expanded locking system or for construction of an incredible cross-Peninsula ship canal which would extend roughly from the AuTrain Basin to Gladstone, Michigan.

Regardless of what eventually happens, precedent is being established and gone forever are the "long ships passing," rather stately examples of the marine architect's artistry. In their place are the graceless, but huge and efficient "motorized barges" of the future...

1. O'Brien, T. Michael, **Guardians of the Eighth Sea, A History of the U.S. Coast Guard on the Great Lakes,** U.S. Government Printing Office, 1976.

2. Such figures should always be closely scrutinized on a case-by-case basis. The incidents very often tend to become inflated.

3. **Daily Mining Journal,** November 26, 1976.

4. As of July 1976, four were stationed (or scheduled to be stationed) on Lake Superior.

5. Under the right conditions, any vessel will ice up — But the 110-footers become particularly unstable with an ice buildup.

6. U.S. Congress, House Committee on Merchant Marine and Fisheries, **Coast Guard Activities on the Upper Great Lakes, Hearings,** before a subcommittee on Coast Guard and Navigation of the Committee on Merchant Marine and Fisheries, House of Representatives, on Oversight Operations in the Upper Great Lakes, 94th Cong., July 16, 1976, p 302.

7. Ibid.

8. This situation is especially critical near Isle Royale, a very popular recreational boating area and a traditionally heavy area of commercial vessel losses.

9. It must be remembered that a degree of "reasonableness" must exist between "safe" ships and Coast Guard rescue capability and owners' profits. Obviously, no vessel can be completely safe, nor can the Coast Guard be everywhere at the same time. A reasonable balance must be achieved.

10. The 44-foot MLB has often been referred to and the mistaken impression might be gained that it is the answer to Lake Superior rescue problems. This is not the case. The 44-foot MLB is a fine boat with great rescue and sea keeping abilities, but like any small craft, there are difficulties associated with its use in heavy weather. The 44-footer is designed much like a cork. With a sealed hull, a self-righting ability and a caged-in crew, it can survive numerous knockdowns and keep on going... But the crew's efficiency suffers under such extreme conditions! When one is out in a wild lake gale in a small craft -- despite certainty in the craft's ability to survive -- your focus centers on the moment. Enormous physical energy is expended "just hanging on" and mental energy is drained as one attempts to comprehend or predict the effect of the next oncoming wave... The cumulative effect is to experience a state of "crew exhaustion" and relative ineffectiveness after a fairly short time. This is a problem with the 44-footers.

11. Correspondence, Ninth District U.S. Coast Guard, 20 Oct. 77.

12. An ideal central Lake Superior location would be the Keweenaw Peninsula.

K.I. Sawyer Air Force Base is scheduled to close in September 1995.

DEPARTMENT OF TRANSPORTATION

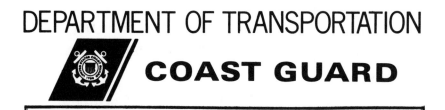

COAST GUARD

MARINE CASUALTY REPORT

SS EDMUND FITZGERALD; SINKING IN LAKE SUPERIOR

ON 10 NOVEMBER 1975 WITH LOSS OF LIFE

(SELECTED PORTIONS ONLY)

U.S. COAST GUARD
MARINE BOARD OF INVESTIGATION REPORT

AND

COMMANDANT'S ACTION

REPORT NO. USCG 16732/64216

DEPARTMENT OF TRANSPORTATION
UNITED STATES COAST GUARD

16732/S.S. EDMUND
FITZGERALD
15 April 1977

From: Marine Board of Investigation
To: Commandant (G–MMI)

Subj: S. S. EDMUND FITZGERALD, O.N. 277437; sinking in Lake Superior on 10 November 1975, with loss of life

Vessel Data

Name:	EDMUND FITZGERALD
Official Number:	277437
Service:	Freight
Gross Tons:	13,632
Net Tons:	8,686
Length (dp):	711 ft.
Length (oa):	729 ft.
Breadth:	75 ft.
Depth:	39 ft.
Propulsion:	Steam Turbine
Horsepower:	7,500
Home Port:	Milwaukee, WI

Owner:	Northwestern Mutual Life Insurance Company, 720 East Wisconsin Ave., Milwaukee, WI 53202
Operator:	Columbia Transportation Div., Oglebay Norton Co., 1210 Hanna Bldg., Cleveland, OH 44115
Master:	Ernest M. McSORLEY Bk 004418 License 398 598, Master and First Class Pilot Steam and Motor Vessels and GT, Master Great Lakes, Connecting and Tributary Waters, First Class Pilot between Duluth, Gary, Buffalo, North Tonawanda and Ogdensburg, Issue 7,9, 29 Oct 1973, Toledo, OH.
Last Inspection for Certification:	9 April 1975, Toledo, OH
Last Spar Deck Inspection:	31 Oct 1975, Toledo, OH
Cargo:	Taconite Pellets, 26,116 long tons
Draft (at departure on last voyage)	27'02" forward 27'06" aft
Propeller Diameter:	19'6"
Pitch (on .7 radius)	15.86'

CONCLUSIONS

1. Preface

The SS EDMUND FITZGERALD left Superior, WI, on the afternoon of 9 November 1975, enroute, Detroit, Mi, with a full cargo of taconite pellets. That evening, and the next day, FITZGERALD proceeded eastward in Lake Superior, on a course north of the charted lanes due to the weather, heading towards Whitefish Bay and the Locks at Sault Ste. Marie, Mi. At the same time, a severe November storm was crossing Lake Superior and, as a result, FITZGERALD encountered worsening weather throughout the early hours of the 10th of November, and by that afternoon, was experiencing winds in excess of 50 knots and seas approaching 16 feet. At approximately 1530 *(3:30 pm)* 10 November, FITZGERALD reported damage, but did not, at that time or in subsequent communications, indicate that it was of a serious nature or that there was any immediate concern for the safety of the vessel. No distress message was received. FITZGERALD sank sometime after 1910 *(7:10 pm)* 10 November 1975, at a position 46° 59.9'N, 85° 06.6'W, approximately 17 miles from the entrance to Whitefish Bay, Mi.

There were no survivors and no witnesses to the casualty. Information available to the Marine Board consists of testimony of people who were on board other vessels in the area at the time FITZGERALD was lost, of people who had served on FITZGERALD prior to its last voyage, of employees of the company which operated the vessel, of other persons familiar with the vessel or similar vessels or its cargo, of personnel of the Coast Guard and of the American Bureau of Shipping who had conducted inspections and surveys on the vessel, of Coast Guard personnel who participated in the extensive search which followed the report of its loss, of personnel from the National Weather Service concerning weather at the time of the loss, of personnel at the facility where the vessel loaded its last cargo, and of information from the several underwater surveys which were conducted on the wreckage which was found on the bottom of Lake Superior.

Information available is incomplete and inconsistent in the following particulars:

a. *Position.* The only information available on the position and trackline of FITZGERALD is in the weather reports sent by FITZGERALD and in testimony of the Master and Watch Officers of the SS ARTHUR M. ANDERSON, which was following FITZGERALD, in voice communication with it, and observing it visually and on radar. The weather reports from FITZGERALD scheduled at 1300 and 1900, *(1:00 and 7:00 pm respectively)*, 10 November, were not received.

The position of FITZGERALD relative to that of ANDERSON cannot be reconstructed. Information available is based on the recollections of the Master and Watch Officers on ANDERSON, since the relative position of FITZGERALD was observed intermittently on the radar, but not recorded. Testimony on these observations is inconsistent. For example, the Officer on watch on ANDERSON recalled that FITZGERALD was "a shade to the right of dead ahead," as FITZGERALD passed northeast of Caribou Island, while the Master thought it was a point to point and a half to the right at that time.

The Master and the Watch Officers on ANDERSON testified at length as to the position and trackline of ANDERSON in the afternoon and evening of 10 November. An analysis of this testimony shows that the vessel was navigated by radar ranges and bearings, that, at times, positions were determined but not logged, that course changes were made without simultaneous determination of position, that positions were determined as much as twenty minutes from the time that course changes were made, and that the courses steered varied from the course logged because of expected drift. The Marine Board attempted to reconstruct the trackline of ANDERSON and found that in order for the vessel to have steered the courses and have been at the positions at the times testified to, the speed of the vessel would have varied from a low of 5 mph to a high of 66 mph. But the

125

Master testified, and the engineering log confirmed, that throughout the period, ANDERSON maintained a steady speed, turning for 14.6 mph. Accordingly, it is concluded that the times and positions reported by officers of ANDER-SON were not sufficiently accurate to allow the trackline of either FITZGERALD or ANDERSON to be reconstructed.

b. *Difficulties Reported by FITZGERALD.* FITZ-GERALD reported the loss of two vents and some fence rail, indicating that topside damage had occurred to the vessel. The flooding which could be expected to result from the loss of any two tank or tunnel vents would not be serious enough, by itself, to cause the loss of the vessel.

FITZGERALD reported, at the same time, that it had developed a list. The existence of the list which would result from flooding of any two ballast tanks, a tunnel, or a tunnel and a ballast tank would not, of itself, indicate damage sufficiently serious to cause the loss of the vessel.

FITZGERALD reported that steps were being taken to deal with the flooding and the list, and that two pumps ("both of them") were being used. FITZGERALD had four 7000-gpm pumps and two 2000-gpm pumps available, indicating that the flooding was evaluated by personnel on board FITZGERALD as not sufficiently serious to create a danger of loss of the vessel.

FITZGERALD reported difficulties with its radars, and requested ANDERSON to provide navigational information.

FITZGERALD reported slowing down to allow ANDER-SON to catch up. This action might have been taken because the Master of FITZGERALD knew or sensed that his problems were of a more serious nature than reported to ANDERSON.

c. *Underwater Survey.* The underwater survey showed that mud covered a majority of the wreckage, that the midships section of the hull was completely disrupted, and that the stern section was inverted. Movement of the survey vehicle disturbed the mud, which limited visibility and made it difficult to survey individual components of the wreckage. However, the survey provided the Marine Board valuable information with respect to the vessel's final condition and orientation.

2. In the absence of more definite information concerning the nature and extent of the difficulties reported and of problems other than those which were reported, and in the absence of any survivors or witnesses, the proximate cause of the loss of the SS EDMUND FITZGERALD cannot be determined.

3. The most probable cause of the sinking of the SS EDMUND FITZGERALD was the loss of buoyancy and stability which resulted from massive flooding of the cargo hold. The flooding of the cargo hold took place through ineffective hatch closures as boarding seas rolled along the Spar Deck. The flooding, which began early on the 10th of November, progressed during the worsening weather and sea conditions and increased in volume as the vessel lost effective freeboard, finally resulting in such a loss of buoyancy and stability that the vessel plunged in the heavy seas.

4. The following factors contributed to the loss of FITZGERALD:

a. The winter load line assigned to FITZGERALD under the changes to the Load Line Regulations in 1969, 1971 and 1973 allowed 3 feet, 3-¼ inches less minimum freeboard than had been allowed when the vessel was built in 1958. This overall reduction in required freeboard also reflected a reduction in Winter Penalty for Great Lakes vessels. Not only did the reduction in minimum required freeboard significantly reduce the vessel's buoyancy, but it resulted in a significantly increased frequency and force of boarding seas in the storm FITZGERALD encountered on 10 November. This, in turn, resulted in an increased quantity of water flooding through loosely dogged hatches and through open-

127

ings from topside damage.

b. The system of hatch coamings, gaskets, covers and clamps installed on FITZGERALD required continuing maintenance and repair, both from routine wear because of the frequent removal and replacement of the covers and from damage which regularly occurred during cargo transfer. That the required maintenance was not regularly performed is indicated by the fact that the crew of the vessel had no positive guidelines, in the form of Company requirements of otherwise, concerning such maintenance. That the required repairs were not regularly performed as damage occurred is indicated by the fact that significant repairs had been required during the previous winter lay-up period and by the fact that more repairs of the same nature were expected, since a general item to repair hatch covers and coamings had been included in the work list for the winter lay-up which FITZGERALD was approaching when it was lost. It is concluded that the system of cargo hatch coamings, gaskets, covers and clamps which was installed on FITZGERALD and the manner in which this system was maintained did not provide an effective means of preventing the penetration of water into the ship in any sea condition, as required by Coast Guard Regulations.

c. Whether all the cargo hatch clamps were properly fastened cannot be determined. In the opinion of the Marine Board, if the clamps had been properly fastened, any damage, disruption or dislocation of the hatch covers would have resulted in damage to or distortion of the clamps. But, the underwater survey showed that only a few of the clamps were damaged. It is concluded that these clamps were the only ones, of those seen, which were properly fastened to the covers and that there were too few of these and too many unfastened or loosely fastened clamps to provide an effective closure of the hatches.

d. The cargo hold was not fitted with a system of sounding tubes or other devices to detect the presence of flooding

The U. S. Coast Guard Underwater Survey of the *Fitzgerald*

So there could be no doubt that this was indeed wreckage of the *Edmund Fitzgerald*, the CURV III photographed her name across the stern – upside down, just as she lies at the bottom. They are in sequence, but are reversed here for benefit of the reader.

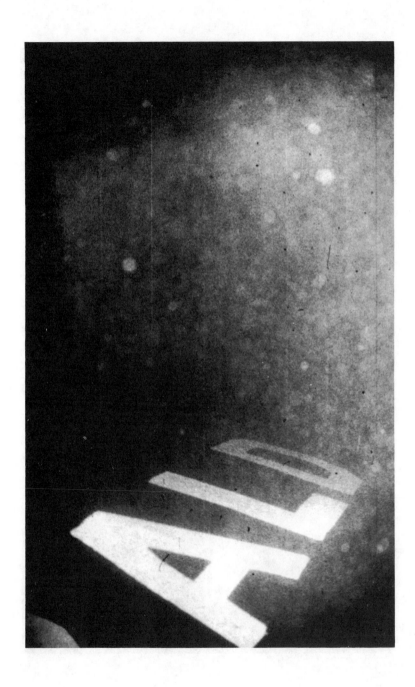

water. It is not known whether any efforts were made to determine if water was entering the cargo hold. If the hold had been checked at a time when the level of water was below the cargo surface, the extent of flooding could not have been determined. It is inconceivable that flooding water in the cargo hold could have reached a height to be seen, without a seasoned Master taking more positive steps for vessel and crew safety than were reported. Therefore, it is concluded that the flooding of the cargo hold was not detected.

e. The cargo hold was not fitted with transverse watertight bulkheads. As a result, the flooding water which entered could migrate throughout the hold, extending the effect of the flooding and aggravating any trim which existed.

5. At sometime prior to 1530 *(3:30 pm)* on 10 November, FITZGERALD experienced damage of sufficient magnitude to cause the Master to report topside damage and a list. Significantly, the Master of the FITZGERALD reported the damage rather than the incident which caused it. It is the opinion of the Marine Board that the incident, while possibly of a serious nature, was not of such extent as to have caused, by itself, the loss of the vessel and, further, that the full extent of the incident was not perceived by vessel personnel. The Master noted the list and topside damage and incorrectly concluded that the topside damage was the only source of flooding. He began what he believed were adequate, corrective measures — pumping spaces which would receive flooding from damaged vents — and thus felt the problems were under control.

The topside damage could have been caused by the vessel striking a floating object which was then brough aboard in the heavy seas. This also could have resulted in undetected damage opening the hull plating above or below the waterline and additional unreported damage to topside fittings, including hatch covers and clamps. Intake of water into the tunnel or into one or more ballast tanks through the damaged vents and open hull would have produced the reported list and increased the rate of cargo hold flooding. The most likely area of damage would have been in the forward part of the ship. The vessel had entered a snow storm approximately one-half hour before the topside damage was reported. In addition, FITZGERALD's radars were reported inoperative shortly after the damage was reported, and may have been malfunctioning for some period before the report. Both the reduced visibility from the snow storm and the radar malfunction would, in the opinion of the Marine Board, have reduced the liklihood that the crew of the vessel could have detected the object in sufficient time to take effective action to avoid it.

The topside damage could have been caused by some unidentified object on board breaking away in the heavy seas. Flooding through such damage could have caused a list. While there were objects on deck which might have come adrift and knocked off a vent cap or damaged a hatch coaming, the only items on deck which had enough mass to do sufficient damage to the hull to cause a sustained list were a hatch cover, the hatch cover crane, or the spare propeller blade. If such extensive damage had occurred, a seasoned Master would have reported it. Such a report was not received.

The topside damage and list could have been caused by a light grounding or near grounding on the shoals north of Caribou Island. Although the testimony is not fully consistent, both the Master and the Watch Officer on ANDERSON indicated that FITZGERALD passed within a few miles of Caribou Island and that they had a conversation concerning the closeness of FITZGERALD to the shoals north of the island. It is considered possible that a light grounding or near grounding on these shoals could have occurred. The vessel could have been damaged from the grounding, from the effect of the violent seas which would be expected near the shoals, or from the shuddering that the vessel would have experienced as it passed near the shoals. The damage could have been on deck, below the water line, or both, leading to the reported topside damage and list. The Marine Board is unable to reconstruct the trackline of FITZGERALD south of Michipicoten Island, however, FITZGERALD was observed to pass two to three miles off Michipicoten Island West End Light from which position a single course change to 141° T would have taken the vessel directly to Whitefish Point on a track well clear of the shoal areas off the northern tip of Caribou. Had there been a delay in making the course change after passing Michipicoten, FITZGERALD would have passed closer to the shoals. But, the distance between Michipicoten and the shoals is such that it appears that a delay in making that course change of upwards of an hour would have been required to cause FITZGERALD to have actually reached the shoals.

The list could have been caused by a localized hull structural failure, resulting in the flooding of a ballast tank or tanks. There is no correlation between such an occurrence and the reported loss of vents and fence rail. The survey of those parts of the wreckage which could be seen showed no evidence of brittle fracture.

The Marine Board concludes that the exact cause of the damage reported cannot be determined, but that the most likely cause was the striking of a floating object.

6. In the opinion of the Marine Board, the flooding from the damage reported, and from other damage which was not detected, most likely occurred in the forward part of the vessel, resulting in trim down by the bow. By the time the damage was reported by FITZGERALD, the flooding of the cargo hold had reached such an extent that the cargo was saturated and loose water existed in the hold. Because of the trim by the bow, this water migrated forward through the non-watertight screen bulkheads which separated the cargo holds, further aggravating the trim and increasing the rate of flooding.

7. Because there were neither witnesses nor survivors and because of the complexity of the hull wreckage, the actual, final sequence of events culminating in the sinking of the FITZGERALD cannot be determined. Whatever the se-

quence, however, it is evident that the end was so rapid and catastrophic that there was no time to warn the crew, to attempt to launch lifeboats or life rafts, to don life jackets, or even to make a distress call.

Throughout November 10th the vessel was subjected to deteriorating weather and an increasing quantity of water on deck. With each wave that came aboard, water found its way into the cargo hold through the hatches. As the vessel lost freeboard because of this flooding and as the sea conditions worsened, the frequency and force of the boarding seas increased, and so did the flooding. The Master of the vessel reported that he was in one of the worst seas he had ever seen. It is possible that, at the time he reported this, FITZGERALD had lost so much freeboard from the flooding of the cargo hold that the effect of the sea was much greater than he would have ordinarily experienced. Finally, as the storm reached its peak intensity, so much freeboard was lost that the bow pitched down and dove into a wall of water and the vessel was unable to recover. Within a matter of seconds, the cargo rushed forward, the bow plowed into the botton of the lake, and the midships structure disintegrated, allowing the submerged stern section, now emptied of cargo, to roll over and override the other structure, finally coming to rest upside-down atop the disintegrated middle portion of the ship.

Alternatively, it is possible that FITZGERALD sank as a result of a structural failure on the surface, resulting from the increased loading of the flooding water. However, this is considered less likely because such a failure would have severed the vessel into two sections on the surface, and one or the other, if not both sections would have floated for a short while. With the weather conditions that existed at the time FITZGERALD was lost and, in particular, with the winds in excess of 50 knots, if either or both of the pieces had floated for any time, significant drifting would have occurred. But the survey of the wreckage showed that the two main pieces were within a ship length, thus little or no drifting took place.

8. There is no evidence that the crew of FITZGERALD made any attempt to use any lifesaving equipment, or that life-saving equipment or its performance contributed in any way to this casualty. The conditions of the lifeboats recovered indicates that the boats were torn away from their chocks, grips and falls. The condition of the life rafts recovered indicates that they were released from their float-free racks and inflated as they were designed to. One raft was damaged, partly when it floated onto the rocky shoreline and partly by a search party which punched holes in it to allow water to drain out during the recovery operation.

Testimony of witnesses indicates that a successful launching of a lifeboat would have been extremely difficult in the weather and sea conditions which prevailed at the time FITZGERALD was lost. This testimony also indicates that Great Lakes mariners have little confidence that lifeboats could be launched successfully in other than moderate wind and sea conditions, and given the choice, they would use the inflatable rafts as the primary means of abandoning a sinking ore carrier. Their confidence in the capability of the rafts was tempered by stated beliefs that a raft could not be boarded safely once it was launched and waterborne and that they would inflate it on deck and wait for it to float free from the sinking vessel. This illustrates that although Great Lakes mariners understand the difficulties inherent in disembarking from a stricken vessel their level of understanding of the use and capability of inflatable life rafts is inadequate. In the opinion of the Marine Board, the appraisal by crewmen that they have small chance of survival on abandoning a stricken vessel in a rough seaway could influence them to stay with the stricken vessel rather than attempt abandonment.

The present requirement for posting a placard containing life raft launching instructions is not considered sufficient to train crewmembers in the proper use of this primary life-saving equipment. The placard is, however, considered a valuable aid in assisting and reinforcing other crew training.

141

Lifeboat drills were held on FITZGERALD during the 1975 season, but were not held on a weekly basis as required by regulations. The level of training of the crew in the use of lifeboats and life rafts is indeterminate.

There is no evidence to indicate that any of the crewmembers of FITZGERALD escaped from the vessel at the time of its loss. However, if they had, their chances of survival would have been significantly enhanced if they had been provided with equipment to protect them against the elements.

9. The twenty-nine crewmen on board FITZGERALD are missing and presumed dead.

10. It was fortunate that the Steamer ARTHUR M. ANDERSON was in the area of and in radiotelephone communication with FITZGERALD on the afternoon and evening of 10 November. Without the presence of this vessel, the loss of FITZGERALD would not have been known for a considerable period of time, possibly not until the following day, and, at the latest, when the vessel failed to arrive at the unloading dock.

11. The testimony of witnesses indicates a conflict as to the time that the Coast Guard was first notified of the problems with FITZGERALD. The Marine Board concludes that the first notification that the Coast Guard received of the problem with FITZGERALD was at approximately 2025 (8:25 pm) Eastern Standard Time on 10 November in a radiotelephone call from CAPT Cooper, Master of ANDERSON. At the time of his call, the actual loss of FITZGERALD was neither comprehended by CAPT Cooper nor conveyed to the Coast Guard. The Coast Guard radio watchstander who received the call attempted to communicate with FITZGERALD, without success, and advised the Rescue Coordination Center. The second call from CAPT Cooper to the Coast Guard, at approximately 2100 (9 pm), 10 November, did express a grave concern that FITZGERALD was lost, and rescue efforts were initiated. It is concluded that the time period which elapsed in evaluating

and reporting the loss of FITZGERALD did not contribute to the casualty or high loss of life, because FITZGERALD sank suddenly, with all hands trapped on board.

12. In the opinion of the Marine Board, in a tragedy of this magnitude, occurring, as this one did, in extreme weather conditions, vessels in the area and SAR aircraft must be relied upon as the first source of assistance.

The response by the merchant vessels in the area to the Coast Guard's request for assistance was in keeping with the finest traditions of mariners. The response of the vessels ARTHUR M. ANDERSON and WILLIAM CLAY FORD is considered exemplary and worthy of special note. These vessels proceeded to the scene on the night of 10 November and searched under conditions of extreme weather and sea on 10 and 11 November. The response of the Canadian vessel HILDA MARJANNE, which got underway but was forced back by weather, is also worthy of note.

The response by Coast Guard SAR aircraft from Air Station Traverse City was timely. The first aircraft was not launched until 51 minutes after it was ordered because it was necessary to load flares for the night search. The launching of three aircraft within one hour and thirty-five minutes is within the response requirements called for by the Ninth Coast Guard District SAR Plan. The request for and dispatch of additional SAR aircraft from Coast Guard Air Station Elizabeth City, NC, from the U.S. Navy, from the Michigan Air National Guard, and from Canadian SAR forces was also timely.

The only Coast Guard surface unit in an SAR standby status which was close enough to respond within a reasonable time and was large enough to cope with the weather and sea conditions which prevailed at the time was the Buoy Tender WOODRUSH at its home port in Duluth, MN. WOODRUSH, on a six-hour standby status, was underway within two and one-half hours. The Marine Board concludes that the response by the WOODRUSH was timely. The wind and sea conditions precluded the use of the Harbor Tug NAUG-ATUCK stationed at Sault Ste. Marie, which had operating limitations imposed on its use outside harbor waters. The small craft designed for coastal operations which were available in Lake Superior were unsuitable for search 15 miles offshore in the high sea state then existing. It is concluded that there is a need for additional surface forces with SAR capability to improve the overall search and rescue posture in Lake Superior.

13. Because ANDERSON was following FITZGERALD, providing navigational assistance and observing FITZGERALD to be on a trackline heading for the entrance to Whitefish Bay and because the wreckage was found on a trackline headed for the entrance to Whitefish Bay, it is concluded that the outages of Whitefish Point light and radio beacon did not contribute to the casualty.

14. The progress of the severe storm which crossed Lake Superior on 9 and 10 November was adequately tracked by the National Weather Service and the weather reports and weather forecasts adequately reflected its path and severity. Weather forecasts were upgraded in a timely manner and a special warning was issued. Estimates of wind velocity by persons on vessels in the storm were higher than those forecast and also higher than those reported by shoreside stations, however, the overall severity of the storm was generally as forecast and reported. It is concluded that mariners on Lake Superior on 10 November were adequately warned of the severe weather and that the Master of FITZGERALD was aware of the severity and location of the storm.

15. Testimony of licensed Great Lakes mariners indicates the cargo hold of a Great Lakes ore carrier cannot be dewatered if it is loaded with a cargo of taconite pellets. The Marine Board is unable to determine the validity of this as a general proposition or whether it affected the loss of FITZ-Gerald.

16. The Loading Manual which was developed for FITZ-

GERALD did not comply with the requirements of the Load Line Regulations. Since the only loading information available to the Marine Board is the total cargo carried on downbound voyages, whether FITZGERALD was ever subjected to unacceptable stresses cannot be determined.

17. The underwater survey of the wreckage and the detailed study of the photographs taken show no apparent relationship between the casualty and the discrepancies found and reported at the Spar Deck Inspection conducted on 31 October, 1975.

18. The hydrographic survey performed by CSS BAYFIELD basically confirmed the data indicated on chart L.S. 9 and CANADIAN chart 2310. In addition, this survey showed that the northern end of the shoals north of Caribou Island extends approximately one mile further east than indicated on Canadian chart 2310.

19. The nature of Great Lakes shipping, with short voyages, much of the time in very protected waters, frequently with the same routine from trip to trip, leads to complacency and an overly optimistic attitude concerning the extreme weather hazards which can and do exist. The Marine Board feels that this attitude reflects itself at times in deferral of maintenance and repairs, in failure to prepare properly for heavy weather, and in the conviction that since refuges are near, safety is possible by "running for it." While it is true that sailing conditions are good during the summer season, changes can occur abruptly, with severe storms and extreme weather and sea conditions arising rapidly. This tragic accident points out the need for all persons involved in Great Lakes shipping to foster increased awareness of the hazards which exist.

20. There is no evidence of actionable misconduct, inattention to duty, negligence, or willful violation of law or regulation on the part of licensed or certified persons, nor evidence that failure of inspected material or equipment, nor evidence that any personnel of the Coast Guard, or any other

145

government agency or any other person contributed to the cause of this casualty.

RECOMMENDATIONS

It is recommended:

1. That Part 45 of Title 46 of the United States Code of Federal Regulations (Great Lakes Load Lines) be amended immediately to rescind the reduction in minimum freeboard brought about by the 1969, 1971 and 1973 changes to the Load Line Regulations.

2. That any subsequent amendments to the Great Lakes Load Line Regulations as they apply to ore carriers, such as FITZGERALD, reflect full consideration of the necessity for a means of detecting and removing flooding water from the cargo hold and for watertight sub-division of the cargo hold spaces. Such an appraisal should take due cognizance of:

    a. The severe weather and sea conditions encountered by these vessels and the resulting high degree of deck wetness, and,

    b. The inherent difficulty in meeting and maintaining a weathertight standard with the system of hatches, coamings, covers, gaskets and clamps used on FITZGERALD and many other Great Lakes vessels.

3. That the owners and operators of Great Lakes ore carrying vessels undertake a positive and continuous program of repair and maintenance to insure that all closures for openings above the freeboard deck are watertight, that is capable of preventing the penetration of water into the ship in any sea condition. This program should include frequent adjustment of hatch clamping devices and vent closures and prompt repair of all hatches, coamings, covers and clamping devices found damaged or deteriorated.

4. That Part 45 of Title 46 of the United States Code of Federal Regulations be amended to require closing and securing of hatches when underway in open waters and closing of vent caps when underway in a loaded condition. A visual inspection of the closure of hatch covers and vent caps should be conducted and logged by a licensed officer prior to sailing in a loaded condition.

5. That the Coast Guard undertake a program to evaluate hatch closures presently used on Great Lakes ore carriers with a view toward requiring a more effective means of closure of such deck fittings.

6. That the owners and operators of Great Lakes vessels, in cooperation with the maritime unions and training schools, undertake a program to improve the level of crew training in the use of lifesaving equipment installed on board the vessels and in other emergency procedures. This program should specifically include training in the use of inflatable life rafts and afford crews of vessels the opportunity to see a raft inflated.

7. That Part 97 of Title 46 of the United States Code of Federal Regulations be amended to require crew training in launching, inflation and operation of inflatable life rafts.

8. That the Coast Guard institute a continuing program of inspections and drills for Great Lakes vessels prior to each severe weather season. The severe weather season should correspond to the Winter Load Line season, i.e., 1 November through 31 March. Under this program, just before the severe weather season began, there would be an inspection to verify that the crew had been trained in the use of the lifesaving equipment and drills would be conducted with the crew then on board the vessel. There would be a physical inspection of the Spar Deck and all critical structural and non-structural members exposed to damage from cargo loading and off-loading equipment including, but not limited to, hatch coamings, hatch covers, vent covers, tank tops, side slopes, hatch-end girders, arches, spar deck stringers, and spar

deck plating. Additionally, all emergency drills would be witnessed, and alarms, watertight closures, navigation equipment and required logs would be inspected.

9. That the Coast Guard take positive steps to insure that the Masters of Great Lakes vessels are provided with information, as is required by the regulations, concerning loading and ballasting of Great Lakes vessels, and that the information provided include not only normal loaded and ballasted conditions, but also details on the sequences of loading, unloading, ballasting and deballasting and the intermediate stages thereof as well as information on the effect upon the vessel of accidental flooding from damage or other sources.

10. That the Coast Guard complete, as soon as possible, the studies, currently underway, which concern primary lifesaving equipment, its launching, and disembarkation from stricken vessels. And, that measures be implemented promptly to improve the entire abandon ship system, including equipping and training personnel, automatic launching of equipment and alerting rescue forces.

11. That the Coast Guard schedule maintenance status for buoy tenders and icebreakers located in the Great Lakes so as to maximize surface search and rescue capability during the severe weather season, consistent with their primary missions.

12. That Subpart 94.60 of Title 46 of the United States Code of Federal Regulations, which requires emergency position indicating radio beacons (EPIRB), be amended to include requirements for such beacons on vessels operating on the Great Lakes during the severe weather season.

13. That the Coast Guard promulgate regulations which require vessels operating on the Great Lakes during the severe weather season to have, for each person on board, a suit designed to protect the wearer from exposure and hypothermia.

14. That navigation charts showing the area immediately

north of Caribou Island be modified to show the extent of the shoals north of the island and that this modification be given the widest possible dissemination, including Notices to Mariners.

15. That the Coast Guard foster and support programs dedicated to increasing awareness, on the part of all concerned with vessel operations, inspection and maintenance, of the hazards faced by vessels in Great Lakes service, particularly during the severe weather season. The programs should make maximum use of company safety programs, safety bulletins, publications and trade journals.

16. That no further action be taken and that this case be closed.

W. W. BARROW, Rear Admiral, USCG
Chairman

A. S. ZABINSKI, Captain, USCG
Member

J. A. WILSON, Captain, USCG
Member

C. S. LOOSMORE, Commander, USCG
Member and Recorder

DEPARTMENT OF TRANSPORTATION
UNITED STATES COAST GUARD

MAILING ADDRESS:
U.S. COAST GUARD (G-MMI/83)
400 SEVENTH STREET SW.
WASHINGTON, D.C. 20590
PHONE (202) 426-1455

Commandant's Action

on

, 2 6 JUL 1977

The Marine Board of Investigation convened to investigate the circumstances surrounding the sinking of the SS EDMUND FITZGERALD in Lake Superior on 10 November 1975 with loss of life

The record of the Marine Board of Investigation convened to investigate the subject casualty has been reviewed; and the record, including the findings of fact, conclusions, and recommendations, is approved subject to the following comments.

REMARKS

1. This casualty presented the Board unique investigative challenges which delayed the submission of the report. Since there were no survivors or witnesses to be questioned, the Board went to considerable lengths to examine wreckage located soon after the casualty. In the spring of 1976, an underwater examination of the wreckage, utilizing highly sophisticated remotely controlled TV and photographic equipment, positively identified the wreck of the SS EDMUND FITZGERALD. The equipment was used to develop a detailed survey and photographic record of the structural damage and position of the wreckage. The sketches of the wreckage in the Board's report, showing the inverted stern section, loose hatch covers, and bow section, were made from this video tape and photographic record.

A further delay in the completion of the final report was due to the time needed to complete the sounding survey, conducted by Canadian authorities, of the water between Michipicoten Island and Caribou Island and adjacent waters.

2. The Commandant concurs with the Board that the most probable cause of the sinking was the loss of buoyancy resulting from massive flooding of the cargo hold. This flooding most likely took place through ineffective hatch closures. As the boarding seas rolled over the spar deck, the flooding was probably concentrated forward. The vessel dove into a wall of water and never recovered, with the breaking up of the ship occurring as it plunged or as the ship struck bottom. The sinking was so rapid and unexpected that no one was able to successfully abandon ship.

With regard to opinions as to the cause of damage and the final sequence of events, an analysis has been made which demonstrates a possibility of capsizing and/or foundering. The analysis of various stages of flooding indicates that bending moment magnitudes and distribution would not support a conclusion of general structural failure as a primary cause of the casualty.

ACTION CONCERNING THE RECOMMENDATIONS

EDITOR'S NOTE —

To avoid needless repetition, the recommendations made on the pages immediately preceding are referred to by number only.

1. The following Board recommendations relate to load line regulations and watertight integrity and are addresses jointly.

Recommendation(s) 1, 3, 4, 5

Action: Assignments of freeboard are based upon, among other things, a presumption of the ability to achieve the watertight integrity necessary to prevent significant flooding.

The mutually dependent areas of safety which are an integral part of all Load Line Regulations are:

a. That the hull is strong enough for all anticipated sea-ways;

b. That the ship is designed and operated with proper stability;

c. That the hull is watertight to the freeboard deck;

d. That the hull has sufficient reserve buoyancy for sea-worthiness;

e. That the topside area is properly fitted so as to be capable of being made weathertight for all anticipated seaways; and,

f. That protection for the movement of the crew on the weather decks at sea is provided.

None of these can be eliminated by additions to freeboard within practical limits. Freeboard, or its increase, is not by itself an adequate substitute for properly designed, main-tained and operated hatches, coamings, gaskets, and securing attachments. Such substitution unduly penalizes good design, maintenance, and operations. Since the fall season of 1976, the Coast Guard has been conducting a Great Lakes Coast Guard ship-rider program to evaluate the overall ef-fectiveness of the combination of freeboard, hatch closure, and ventilator closure effectiveness during the Intermediate (Oct 1 –31) and Winter (November 1 – March 31) freeboard seasons. This program has confirmed the evidence found by the Board of Investigation indicating that it is not a singular occurrence that the hatch covers on the EDMUND FITZ-GERALD may not have been properly secured. Several ships have been found to suffer in varying degrees from a lack of weathertight integrity due to the inability to make hatch covers watertight and due to the inattention to ventilator covers prior to a winter season voyage.

Accordingly, the Commandant is initiating action to:

a.   Continue the ship-rider program in 1977 and in suc-ceeding years as necessary in order to prevent sailing or severely restrict the voyage weather limits of any ship found to lack sufficient watertight integrity. Extra seasonal free-board requirements may also be assigned to supplement

Various Coast Guard Surface Units and Aircraft
Which Figured in the *Fitzgerald* Affair

ONTARIO

MICHIPICOTEN IS.

CARIBOU
IS.

ERIOR

FITZGERALD
LAST SEEN?

WRECK ✕

COPPER MINE
POINT

17 mi.

WHITEFISH PT.

WHITEFISH
BAY

GRAND
MARAIS

SAULT STE. MARIE

PER PENINSULA

MICHIGAN

weather limitations by the Commander, Ninth Coast Guard District to vessels on an individual basis.

b.   Bring to the attention of the owners and operators the fact that weathertight closures which are not effective when battened down void both the LOAD LINE CERTIFICATE and the CERTIFICATE of INSPECTION.

c.   Firmly bring to the attention of ships' masters their operational responsibilities for weathertight integrity before and during weather conditions as outlined in operational regulations in 46 CFR 97.

d.   Direct the Merchant Marine Technical Divisions at Coast Guard Headquarters, in cooperation with Commander, Ninth Coast Guard District, to immediately undertake a critical evaluation of the effectiveness of those hatch closures presently in use on Great Lakes bulk carriers utilizing information from the shipboard Coast Guard inspections. If requiring such maintenance as to be difficult to assure weathertight integrity, regulatory notices will be published stating their design or maintenance shortcomings and include a requirement that ships modify or change hatch covers to correct the deficiencies.

e.   Direct the Merchant Marine Technical Division to reassess the existing INTERMEDIATE and WINTER Season freeboard corrections utilizing wave analysis information on Great Lakes wave spectra to be gathered during an ongoing research program (1977–1979).

2.   The following recommendation concerns vessel subdivision and is relevant to the preceding Action.

Recommendation 2: a & b

Action: The Commandant intends to develop a federal regulation establishing a minimum level of subdivision for inspected Great Lakes cargo ships for two reasons directly related to this casualty.   First, the sudden catastrophic

161

foundering of the vessel apparently allowed no time for radio messages nor for individual survival. Second, the SS EDMUND FITZGERALD survived for several hours *after* indicating by radio message that some damage had occurred and the ship was about one hour from a safe harbor when it sank.

It is possible that even a minimum degree of watertight subdivision within the cargo hold could have effected a great change on the ultimate fate of both the ship and her crew. It is possible that the flooding, which is presumed to have occurred through ineffective hatch covers, might have occurred through only 1 or 2 hatches, but the subsequent flooding was able to penetrate the entire cargo hold. Subdivision bulkheads in the cargo space would have limited this flooding, possibly enough to allow the ship to make it to safe harbor. If they had realized the extent of damage, the provision of subdivision calculations and damage control instructions might have at least allowed the crew more time to escape prior to the sinking.

An additional concern is raised by the report of minor side damage incidents. Bulk carriers are now being built which do not have the crew passage, ballast tank combination at the sides which provided some protection in cases of minor penetration. The arrangements on these new vessels are such that a penetration of the hull near the waterline might cause flooding over 90% of the ship's length. An incident could occur such that little chance of preventing sinking of the vessel would exist and the crew might have a very short time to escape. Subdivision standards will be directed toward this type of casualty. As the benefits of subdivision apply also to oceangoing cargo ships, international discussion toward an increase in subdivision safety for all cargo ships will be further pursued.

3. The following recommendations concern lifesaving equipment and crew training and are addressed jointly.

Recommendations 6, 7, 8, 10, 13 & 15

Action: The intent of these recommendations is concurred with and the need for improved and periodic meaningful training in the use of lifesaving equipment and a vessel readiness inspection program prior to severe weather sailing is supported. The following action has been taken or will be taken relative to these recommendations:

a. In October 1976, the Coast Guard instituted a continuing program of inspections and drills for Great Lakes vessels prior to the severe weather season. The scope of the program includes specific items listed in Recommendation 8 and the inspections are conducted while the vessels are underway and under actual operational conditions.

The requirements for conducting emergency drills and crew training are contained in 46 CFR Parts 97.15-35 and 97.13-20. Emergency fire and boat drills are required at least once every week and the master is responsible to assure that they are conducted. Assuring adequate drills are conducted is not unique to Great Lakes vessels, therefore the operations sections of 46 CFR, Parts 35, 78, 167 and 185 will be amended to incorporate crew training in the launching, inflation, and operation of inflatable life rafts. The Coast Guard recognizes this lack of training is of international magnitude and is working within IMCO in the preliminary stages of such a program.

b. Owners, operators, labor organizations, and training schools will be encouraged to develop a training program of the type indicated in Recommendation 6. To support this effort, the Merchant Vessel Personnel Division will work with the Maritime Administration to develop such training programs. The Coast Guard will set qualification standards requiring all licensed officers and able seamen be trained in the operation of inflatable life rafts as well as other lifesaving equipment. Input from the owners and operators of Great Lakes vessels, along with their crews' labor organizations and training schools, will be solicited.

c. The Coast Guard is expanding its public awareness program to provide useful information to seamen and aid operators and unions in the conduct of their training programs. In September 1975, a pamphlet on hypothermia, CG-473, was published and distributed on the Great Lakes and other areas where cold weather survival could be a problem. A proposal has been submitted within the Coast Guard to the Office of Research and Development to develop a means by which the public, specifically those on board commercial vessels, will be made aware of various safety factors, regulations, and safe operating procedures that apply to their particular commercial operation. For example, pamphlets may be developed and distributed (i.e. , via labor unions, commercial fisherman organizations, vessel documentation officers, professional and business organizations) for each class of commercial operation. Great Lakes vessels would be an appropriate area for such a public awareness program.

A summary of the Board's report and an article, directed at increasing the mariner's awareness of the hazards of the Great Lakes, will be prepared for publication in the Proceedings of the Marine Safety Council.

Concerning Recommendations 10 and 13, a Notice of Proposed Rulemaking based on an Advance Notice of Proposed Rulemaking, published 7 June 1976 in the Federal Register, is being prepared for Great Lakes cargo, tank, and passenger vessels which will propose that:

    a.   All lifeboats on vessels be totally enclosed to provide protection from exposure and to lessen the danger of swamping and subsequent capsizing.

    b.   All lifeboats be diesel engine driven with the ability to start the engine in temperatures as low as $-22°$ F.

    c.   Sufficient lifeboats be provided to accommodate 100% of the persons on board the ship with additional lifeboats and life rafts provided and located so as to provide accommodation for an additional 100% in the event that a casualty renders the other lifeboats unusable.

   d.   All survival craft be provided with launching devices which will be launched from their stowed positions with all persons onboard, eliminating the need for lengthy prelaunch preparations, a deck crew to stay aboard to control the launch, and in the case of life rafts, the need to enter the water before boarding.

   e.   Automatic float-free launching be required for life rafts.

   f.   An exposure suit be required for each person on board that will protect the wearer from exposure and hypothermia.

One lifeboat manufacturer is developing a float-free launching system for lifeboats which are also launched conventionally. This will be given further consideration as a requirement upon completion of a prototype system and an evaluation of its feasibility.

The remainder of the Board's recommendations are addressed individually.

4. Recommendation 9:

   Action: The Coast Guard will develop performance criteria for loading manuals which will cover all the items in this recommendation except flooding conditions. Flooding conditions will be addressed in conjunction with the casualty control efforts discussed in the action on Recommendation 2.

5. Recommendation 11:

   Action: Commander, Ninth Coast Guard District has implemented this recommendation by issuing a District Directive on 9 September 1976. This Directive contains the requirements and guidelines for scheduling maintenance and underway periods of Coast Guard vessels on the Great Lakes.

6. Recommendation 12:

Action:　Action is being taken to permit the operation of EPIRB's in the VHF-FM marine band. There is at present virtually complete shore station coverage on the Great Lakes on this band and constant monitoring of Channel 16 by stations in both the United States and Canada. A prototype EPIRB for testing is now being developed by the Transportation Systems Center. When the VHF – FM EPIRB's become available, regulations will be proposed requiring that they be installed on board inspected Great Lakes vessels during all seasons.

7. Recommendation 14:

Action:　A copy of the completed marine casualty report will be forwarded to the U.S. Department of Commerce, National Oceanic and Atmospheric Administration, with a request that they coordinate the correction of the applicable charts with their counterparts in the Canadian Government.

O. W. SILER
Admiral, U. S. Coast Guard
Commandant

LAKE CARRIERS' ASSOCIATION

ROCKEFELLER BUILDING
CLEVELAND, OHIO 44113
(216) 621-1107

September 16, 1977

Mr. Webster B. Todd, Jr.
Chairman
National Transportation Safety Board
800 Independence Avenue, S.W.
Washington, D.C. 20594

Subject:　　Coast Guard Investigation Report dated
July 26, 1977 on FITZGERALD sinking

Dear Mr. Chairman:

The lake shipping industry, proud of its safety record through the years, completely rejects the Coast Guard theoretical cause of the FITZGERALD sinking. We are setting forth the basis for our position and urge that our statement be considered in your deliberations in the case.

Lake Carriers' Association consists of 15 domestic bulk shipping companies on the lakes. 135 vessels are involved with a registered gross of 1,395,065 tons.

Owners and operators have a paramount interest in navigation safety. In addition to their prime asset, an experienced crew, there is significant investment in the vessel and value of any cargo on board. Where changes in design or regulations are found necessary from operating experience or casualties, there is no question as to a corrective course of action. When changes running into millions of dollars are recommended based only on a *possible* cause of an accident, industry most vigorously objects. And further, when the possibility is poorly supported by known factors, industry is even more upset.

In its conclusions, the Coast Guard Marine Board stated: "....... the proximate cause of the loss of the S/S EDMUND FITZGERALD cannot be determined."

In his action on the Board's findings, conclusions and recommendations, the Commandant stated: "With regard to opinions as to the cause of damage and the final sequence of events, an analysis has been made which demonstrates a possibility of capsizing and/or foundering. The analysis of various stages of flooding indicates that bending moment magnitudes and distribution would not support a conclusion of general structural failure as a primary cause of the casualty."

"The Commandant concurs with the Board that the most probable cause of the sinking was the loss of buoyancy resulting from massive flooding of the cargo. hold. This flooding most likely took place through ineffective hatch closures. As the boarding seas rolled over the spar deck, the flooding was probably concentrated forward. The vessel dove into a wall of water and never recovered, with the breaking up of the ship occurring as it plunged or as the ship struck the bottom. The sinking was so rapid and unexpected that no one was able to successfully abandon ship."

It should be emphasized that the proximate cause of the sinking could not be determined, so any theoretical rationale advanced could only be a *possible* cause. Thereafter the recommendations of the Board with general approval of the Commandant proceed on structural and hatch closure details with specificity as if the actual cause of sinking had been determined.

The Coast Guard has pointed its finger at ineffective hatch closures as the most likely cause of the sinking. Let's examine that thesis, then look at another much more likely cause.

The present hatch covers are an advanced design and are considered by the entire lake shipping industry to be a most significant improvement over the telescoping leaf covers previously used for many years. The one piece covers have proven completely satisfactory in all-weather operations without a single vessel loss in almost 40 years of use. Closure clamps have been greatly improved over the years to the present cast steel clamps that have also been found to be completely satisfactory in service.

Raised coamings that support the hatch covers on non-self-unloading vessels sustain minor damage from time to time by shore based unloading equipment. It is necessary to have periodic repairs and strengthening done on such vessels. The Board noted that some work was scheduled for the FITZGERALD at her next shipyard availability. But the Board failed to note that this is an annual winter layup work item for most straight deck vessels, such as the FITZGERALD, depending upon the unloading docks traded at. The FITZGERALD was in a trade that involved much less damage than many other similar vessels. There was nothing unusual about this repair item on the next shipyard work list. It is important to note that the spar deck inspection of the FITZGERALD, conducted ten days before the sinking by the Coast Guard OCMI at Toledo and the American Bureau of Shipping, the classification society relied upon by the Coast Guard, revealed no significant damage of the hatch coamings or closure fittings.

We call attention to almost forty years' experience with the current type of hatch covers and closure clamps that have been improved during the period. If ineffective closings exist, as alleged by the Coast Guard, surely during the forty years operating experience there would have been watery cargo to unload, be it ore, coal, grain or stone. This not only would have been readily apparent, but also a costly problem that vessel and cargo owners would not tolerate. If significant water did enter the cargo holds in this manner during a downbound voyage there would be a corresponding change in draft. Draft readings are recorded by the vessel before leaving the loading port, by the Corps of Engineers at the Soo Locks and by the vessel upon arrival at the unloading port. Periodically the Coast Guard checks the drafts. There are few unexplained changes that have occurred enroute, and none of these were accompanied by water accumulation in the cargo holds . . . in over almost forty years of experience.

The Board has pointed to improper hatch closure procedures being observed on other vessels to support the contention that those on the FITZGERALD probably were not closed properly. We submit that there is no validity to such imputation theory. What might have been observed on one or more vessels in other than heavy weather conditions should under no circumstances be assumed to have been the case on the FITZGERALD in the weather she was experiencing. Consequently, we question the Coast Guard's conclusion on hatch closure procedures.

The Master of the ANDERSON reported that his vessel and the FITZGERALD had proceeded more or less together across Lake Superior at their normal speeds. Based on weather forecasts and deteriorating northeasterly weather, they both worked up to the lee of the Canadian shore as they proceeded eastward. At 0953 *(9:53 am)* the ANDERSON reported that the vessels were not taking any green water aboard, only spray. At 1152 *(11:52 am)* the ANDERSON again reported that conditions were normal. In eastern Lake Superior on the afternoon of November 10, as the vessels changed course to pass between Michipicoten and Caribou Islands, the wind started hauling around to the south and eventually to the northwest.

At 1520 *(3:20 pm)* the Second Mate logged ANDERSON abeam Michipicoten Island West End Light at a distance of 7.7 miles. The seas were beginning to build rapidly from the northwest and the Master changed course to 125°. This new course was "shaped up" to clear Six Fathom Shoal north of Caribou Island and to reach a point 8 miles off the island. The FITZGERALD was 17 miles ahead and to the right of dead ahead. The FITZGERALD was then observed to open further to the right of ANDERSON's heading. This would have put the FITZGERALD in the vicinity of the Six Fathom Shoals area. The Master of the ANDERSON testified at the Coast Guard inquiry that he had told the Mate on watch that the FITZGERALD was closer to this shoal than he wanted the ANDERSON to be. No plot of the FITZGERALD was maintained.

When the FITZGERALD departed Superior (Wisconsin) on November 10 her draft was 27 feet, 2 inches forward and 27 feet, 6 inches aft. The Master of the ANDERSON reported 10-15 foot waves experienced above Caribou Island

170

and as high as 25 feet below Caribou as the seas built up from the northwest winds coming across the lake. Steady winds as high as 43 knots were recorded by the ANDERSON at 1520 *(3:20 pm)*; winds at 58 knots were logged at 1652 *(4:52 pm)*.

Bewteen 1530 and 1535 *(3:30 and 3:35 pm)*, or 10 to 15 minutes after the FITZGERALD was observed by the ANDERSON to be in the Six Fathom area, the FITZGERALD advised the ANDERSON of a list, some fence rail damage and the loss of two ballast tank vents. The FITZGERALD advised she was slowing down to permit the ANDERSON to catch up and keep track of her. She also reported that both of her pumps were going. Presumably this meant two 7,000 GPM ballast pumps. It was not until 1610 or 1615 *(4:10 or 4:15 pm)* that the FITZGERALD advised her radars were not working and asked the ANDERSON to provide navigational assistance. Note that this does not establish just when the radars became inoperative.

It should be emphasized that minutes after passing Six Fathom Shoal FITZGERALD reported a list, two ballast tank vents had carried away and that two ballast pumps were in use. Capacity of the two pumps was 14,000 gallons per minute. Each vent opening in the deck would be eight inches in diameter, so the amount of water entering two eight-inch vents could readily have been handled by the ballast pumps. With the two pumps operating there should have been no list from this source of water, particularly in as short of time as 10 to 15 minutes. Captain Cooper of the ANDERSON testified that "he took that list which seemed to be real fast." Within the time frame involved, such a list can only be readily explained by holing of the vessel's ballast tanks caused by striking Six Fathom Shoals.

It should be noted that there was no report of hatch damage or hatches opening up. Water on the main deck would have resulted in a compressive action, pushing the hatch covers more tightly on their gaskets, rather than lifting them. There was no indication water was entering the holds from topside other than the small amount coming through the two openings. It should be kept in mind that the hatch covers are on coamings raised two feet above the main

171

deck.

Had the water causing the list been entering the cargo hold from the topside the amount of water passing aft to the cargo hold suction would have been insufficient to support even one ballast pump. It is also questionable whether water in the cargo hold would have resulted in a list since it would not have been restricted to one side of the vessel. Moreover, if flooding commenced in the forward part ɔf the vessel and forward trim were affected, as theorized by the Coast Guard, the suction point, which is located in the after cargo hold, would have been elevated and pumping would not have been possible. Yet the vessel had two pumps going and the Master reported the FITZGERALD was holding her own at that time, which indicated that water was being pumped and *could not have come through the cargo holds!!* The damage then had to be on the bottom and, since there was no indication of any structural failure, must have been caused by an external force such as shoaling.

Considering that the vessels had only been underway for a day, that no damage or abnormally severe weather was experienced up to the early afternoon on November 10, that no mention was made of hatch cover damage or loss, it becomes all too apparent that the quantity of water needed to sink the FITZGERALD could not have seeped through the hatch covers.

After the initial damage caused by shoaling, the vessel labored in heavy quartering seas for over three hours as it proceeded towards Whitefish Point. Thus, excessive working from rolling and pitching was inevitable, accompanied by progressive extension of the initial damage. As the vessel filled up gradually from the bottom to the point where its buoyancy was marginal, a large wave or series of heavy waves could have raised the stern, starting the bow's dive underwater, never to recover. Since the pilothouse was on the bow it would have gone under immediately, leaving no opportunity to alert the crew or radio for help.

The Marine Board indicated that taconite pellets can absorb up to 7 percent moisture. Without explanation this information is "illusive". Under optimum conditions, pellets can contain up to 7 percent moisture, the average a-

172

mount is less. Not stated is the fact that they contain 3 to 5 percent in the stockpile and when loaded in the cargo holds. Under exposure to moisture they can perhaps absorb 1 or 2 percent *more over a period of time.* There have been statements by the Coast Guard that the pellet cargo could soak up 2,000 tons of water and leave no telltale moisture in the bottom of the hold.

Hatch covers could have been blown off by the compressed air in the cargo compartments as water entered from the sides or the bottom. This is a well-known phenomenon based on experience in vessel sinkings. Or hatch covers could have sprung from the weight of pellets as the vessel dove to the bottom. These same actions would have sprung or broken hatch clamps. Contrary to the Board's findings, the underwater pictures do not support a conclusion that the hatch clamps were not closed properly.

The Coast Guard indicated that a study would be undertaken to determine whether present system for hatch closures on lake vessels can be improved. The industry is always interested in improved equipment or procedures, so such a study is supported.

If the ineffective hatch closure theory is not plausible, then what is likely to have happened? The Coast Guard quickly dismissed the possibility of shoaling near Caribou Island. The reason given was that an accurate track in that area could not be determined from the ANDERSON officers' testimony. Indeed, there was a lack of preciseness that would have been invaluable in proving or disproving the shoaling theory. The ANDERSON's Master, having no inkling of serious trouble on the FITZGERALD, did not record the position of either vessel. Even though not recorded at the time, this experienced Master nonetheless determined from his observations that the FITZGERALD had passed through the Six Fathom (36 feet) Shoal area near Caribou Island. After the fact, when the FITZGERALD was known to be lost, he did not broadcast the information by radio, but made a "confidential" report to his home office by telephone at the first opportunity. His report was taped by the home office.

The Master of the ANDERSON did not volunteer that information when he first appeared as a witness in the Inquiry but the tape was subsequently offered to the Board by his company because of its pertinency to the hearing.

(The following two paragraphs did not appear in the Lake Carriers' Association original statement of September 16, 1977. According to John A. Packard, Secretary of the Lake Carriers' Association, they have been added to the original statement in an effort to amplify points made therein. We have indicated the added paragraphs with brackets.)

[The navigation position data near Caribou Island furnished by the Master of the ANDERSON is materially strengthened by direct radar observations, in contrast to the confusing reconstructed track line produced by the Marine Board. On page 2149 of the Board Report, Captain Cooper stated he simultaneously had *both* the FITZGERALD and Caribou on his radar, and he was positive that the FITZGERALD went over the shoals. Captain Cooper meticulously avoided the shallower waters because of the heavy seas normal there in such storm conditions.

The significant point is the simultaneous radar observation of Caribou and the vessel. When one object is fixed (Caribou), the distance can be rather accurately determined without any concern for relative motion, bearings, track lines, position, speed or heading. The radar is equipped with concentric ring scales enabling the experienced observer to estimate distances between objects on its screen.]

The result of the hydrographic survey of the Caribou Island shoal waters conducted by Canadian Hydrographic Service, at the request of the Coast Guard Marine Board looking into the FITZGERALD sinking, is described on Pages 86 and 87 of the Report. It should be particularly noted that the survey identifies a shoal less than six fathoms deep more than one mile farther east than any in the Six Fathom Shoal cluster depicted on the latest navigation charts. This verified shoal was in the track of the FITZGERALD, as observed by the ANDERSON, thus making shoaling even more certain as the start of the fateful events leading to the sinking. This fact should be considered along with the taped report of the ANDERSON's Master.

Loadline changes . . . In view of the foregoing, and since the Marine Board found there was no structural failure, nor has any experience or data been cited showing that 1969, 1971 or 1973 changes in the Loadline Regulations were improper or unwise, this recommendation should be dismissed.

To qualify for a reduction in freeboard the Coast Guard has imposed a group of conditions that enhance ship' safety. Only those ships which incorporated certain structural features were eligible to take advantage of the specified draft increases. For example, in 1969, for a 600' ship to gain 5.5 inches of draft it would have to be constructed in compliance with recently upgraded ABS [1] rules; have steel, one-piece, watertight hatch covers - instead of boards and tarpaulins; have steel deckhouses; be proven structurally suitable for the resulting loaded draft in all operating conditions; and have under deck passages, or tunnels, permitting personnel to move fore and aft in safety.

There has been an implication that a ship receives a loadline assignment precisely calculated in accord with the structural stresses imposed by the deadweight corresponding to the loadline draft. Ignored is the fact that the scantlings used must satisfy a number of criteria, including the imperical - and generally conservative rules of a classification society. The truth is that, in the first instance, a vessel's freeboard is set by its length, depth, deck height or sheer pattern, extent and staunchness of superstructures and deckhouses, and the efficacy of a number of fittings such as watertight closures, freeing ports and means of protecting the crew. Then, it must be proven that the structural strength is commensurate with the loads corresponding to that freeboard draft.

In every instance, when a ship seemingly becomes eligible for a freeboard decrease by reason of a subsequent amendment to the loadline regulations, it is necessary to prove to the Coast Guard and the classification society that the vessel's structure measures up to deeper loading. At this time, furthermore, many details of structure and equipment come under the scrutiny of these regulatory agencies with the result that they are generally — and expensively — upgraded. Thus it may be seen that decreased freeboard or increased draft is not a present lightly bestowed by the Coast Guard, rather, *quid pro quo* in the form of safety enhancement is demanded for these allegedly perilous inches.

Watertight compartmentation . . . Some background may be helpful to counter the thinking that lake vessels have no watertight compartments and are merely one large "bathtub".

Great Lakes vessels are designed by competent naval architects based on criteria developed and published by one of the worldwide classification societies (American Bureau of Shipping and Lloyds Registry on the Great Lakes) and the regulations of the United States or Canadian Coast Guard. Additionally, a proposed design must be submitted and approved by both a classification society and the governmental regulatory authority. The basic strength standard and the loadline assigned a vessel is in accordance with international regulation under joint agreement of the United States and Canadian governments.

Great Lakes vessels are designed with segregated ballast tanks. This means that the ship has tanks designed exclusively for water ballast and it is not necessary to utilize the cargo hold for water ballast when in the light condition. These tanks provide a double shell over the entire bottom of the cargo hold and vertically up the sides to about the loaded water line on most ships. Tunnels under the weather deck have watertight doors and afford watertight integrity several feet above the main deck. However, the envelope extends to the weather deck on some designs. The typical Great Lakes bulk vessel has six to nine ballast tanks on each side. Each tank is divided port and starboard by a watertight bulkhead. Additionally, the ship is divided into complete watertight compartments by the collision bulkhead forward and the engine room bulkhead aft. Afterpeak tanks are watertight and extend vertically to one deck below the weather deck.

These watertight subdivisions and ballast tanks afford a substantial margin of safety in case the shell of the vessel is penetrated allowing water to flood one or more of these compartments. Damage control can be exercised through the use of a combination of ballast pumps, compressed air applied to the tanks and use of the collision tarps.

A claim has been made that while lake vessels may lack watertight subdivisions between cargo holds, ocean going vessels are required to have watertight bulkheads between cargo spaces. Actually there is no basic requirement for a seagoing *cargo* ship to have any watertight subdivision beyond the collision bulkhead, machinery space bulkhead(s) and the afterpeak bulkhead. Further subdivision to meet floodability criteria is required only when freeboard less than "Steamer" or Type "B" freeboard is desired.

Since 1970 vessels built under Title XI Mortgage Insurance Procedures are required to have "one compartment" watertight stability. Whether or not required, our members are moving towards improved watertight compartmentation in new construction. Accomplished in that manner, the cost is not prohibitive, as compared to retrofitting.

In a further effort, and in the light of the foregoing, Maritime Administration has recently invited bids on a contract to consider the practicality of further watertight compartmentation on lake vessels.

Lake shipping safety in general . . . A few additional comments will update the status and progress of our safety efforts. At the House Merchant Marine and Fisheries Committee Coast Guard oversight hearings at the Soo on July 16, 1976, I listed a number of steps under consideration by government and industry that would, in my opinion, be a quantum step forward safety-wise.

Hull monitoring . . . First is the development of a hull monitoring system with an appropriate pilothouse readout to interpret hull actions in all-weather situations and to alert the master that trouble is developing. No matter what survival systems are available for the vessel personnel, if they don't know they are in trouble, such as was apparently the case on the FITZGERALD, safety will not prevail. A contract is in process by MARAD to pull available technology together to develop and test such a monitoring system on a lake vessel. Much of the preliminary stress measurement procedures have already been accomplished on lake vessels.

Develop an all-weather capsule . . . In my opinion, lifeboats, as we have known them through the years, are obsolescent today. This is not only because of current technology, but also reduced professionalism in today's seamen.

We have recommended a change in Coast Guard regulations to permit development and use of survival equipment other than the traditional life rafts and lifeboats. The changes are still under consideration. There is not much incentive for such investment until the future is clarified.

Since recommending development of a "survival capsule" for shipboard use, interest has been expressed by several firms in this country. And in Norway, government, shipping and classification society authorities have developed a 36-man capsule that can be ejected from a ship's deck. This is especially advantageous where fire or other hazardous cargoes are involved. Our cargoes on the lakes don't fall into this category, so we are more interested in a capsule that can be boarded in all-weather and can float free if the vessel sinks.

Survival suits . . . On August 11, 1977, after considerable study, the Coast Guard approved two survival suits for shipboard use. This eliminated the liability problem in using lifesaving equipment that does not have Coast Guard approval.

Improved weather forecasting . . . A number of changes are underway that should result in improved marine weather forecasting for the lakes. Weather buoys, the assignment of marine forecasters, more vessels reporting weather data, looking at the lakes as a weather system for marine purposes and better communications are under consideration or in process. This, together with improved meterological training of deck officers, will further enhance safety of lake shipping.

Position keeping on the lakes . . . Since it is now almost certain that the FITZGERALD grounded on a shoal above

Caribou Island, and there is no evidence of structural failure, we must conclude there was a navigational problem, not a design weakness nor a hatch closure deficiency.

What was the navigation problem and how can we minimize it for other vessels?

We know that the FITZGERALD advised the ANDERSON at 1610 to 1615 *(4:10 to 4:15 pm)* that his radars were not working and asked for navigation assistance. But we don't really know just when the radars went out nor how. Did both go at the same time from a large wave action? Where was the vessel in relation to the Six Fathom Shoals area above Caribou?

The east side of Caribou Island is relatively low so wave action would have distorted radar signals giving an impression of being farther from the island than was actually the case. The radio beacon at Whitefish Point was not operating. Bearings from this beacon would have indicated the vessel's position east or west of the shoal area. This signal would have been especially critical under the circumstances involved.

Two changes are underway that will improve navigation in the future, one will be especially helpful. As part of the national navigation plan, Loran-C coverage for the lakes is to be provided by the Coast Guard by 1980; This remarkably accurate position finding system is not affected by visibility, sea return or other weather conditions. It will be the principal means of navigation, complementing radar, and will obsolete radio beacons on the lakes. Consequently, completion of the Loran-C coverage should be expedited.

The other change is a requirement for fathometers on lake vessels. The bottom characteristics of the lakes and the limited bottom information shown on charts will limit the usefulness of this equipment, but it may be of some help in special situations.

And finally, the uncharted shoal *less* than six fathoms deep over one mile east of Six Fathom Shoal north of Caribou Island will be shown on future navigation charts of eastern Lake Superior.

— — — — —

Mr. Chairman, the lake shipping industry and its professional naval architect advisors can find NOTHING in the available factors to support the Coast Guard's thesis that the sinking resulted from poor hatch closure procedures. We can't identify one such factor, whereas, such factors do support shoaling as the cause of the sinking.

If we can provide any other information or assistance, please call on us.

Respectfully submitted,

LAKE CARRIERS' ASSOCIATION

Paul E. Trimble
Vice Admiral USCG (Ret.)
President

EDITOR'S NOTE —

Italics have been used to denote those words underscored in the Lake Carriers' Statement of September 16. The time conversions, also in italics, were added for the benefit of the reader. Footnotes (not appearing in the original statement) have also been added by the editors.

1. ABS - American Bureau of Shipbuilders

AND THE TALE CONTINUES!

Since the original publication of this book in December of 1977, additional information concerning the catastrophic loss of the FITZGERALD has come to light. None of this information significantly contradicts the previous material, but it does provide insight and understanding of both the loss of the vessel and the general SAR (Search And Rescue) situation on Lake Superior.

One might have thought that after the extensive Coast Guard investigation and the lengthy Lake Carriers Association counter report, the last "official word" was heard; that all that would follow would be mindless speculation. Not true. There still was the investigation and report by the National Transportation Safety Board (NTSB). Kay Bailey, at the time (1977), the Acting Chairman, explained the Board's role thusly: "Under Public Law 93-633, 49 USC 1901, "Independent Safety Board Act of 1974," the National Transportation Safety Board was given broad responsibilities for the promulgation of transportation safety by conducting accident investigations and formulating safety improvement recommendations."

"To comply with the requirements of the statute and to efficiently utilize the resources of the government while simultaneously maintaining an independent overview of marine accident investigations, joint NTSB-Coast Guard regulations have been formulated. Under these regulations, the NTSB report of a major marine accident may be based upon a NTSB conducted investigation and hearing. Alternatively, NTSB may request the Coast Guard to conduct an investigation with NTSB participation and the evidentiary material produced is used to compile the NTSB report which is issued to the public. The Coast Guard conducts an investigation for its own purposes in either case."

"The FITZGERALD accident occurred during a transition from past procedures to the present procedure described above. Formerly the NTSB was charged with the determination of probable cause and a single combined report was issued." [1]

The NTSB didn't simply "rubber stamp" the Coast Guard report, rather they ranged far and wide in conducting a deliberate rational investigation. On May 4,1978, two and a half years after the tragic loss, the NTSB issued its report. [2]

The Coast Guard concluded that the "most probable cause" of the sinking was the loss of buoyancy and stability which resulted from massive flooding of the cargo hold. The flooding of the cargo hold took place through ineffective hatch closures as boarding seas rolled along the spar deck. The flooding . . . progressed during the worsening weather and sea conditions had increased in volume as the vessel lost effective freeboard, finally resulting in such a loss of buoyancy and stability that the vessel plunged in the heavy seas."[3]

The NTSB disagreed, stating that "the probable cause . . . was the sudden massive flooding of the cargo hold due to the collapse of one or more hatch covers. Before the hatch covers collapsed, flooding into the ballast tanks and tunnel through nonweathertight hatch covers caused a reduction in freeboard and a list. The hydrostatic and hydrodynamic forces imposed on the hatch covers by heavy boarding seas at this point reduced freeboard and with the list, caused the hatch covers to collapse."[4]

The key word is *SUDDEN*. The NTSB concluded it was the "sudden massive flooding due to the collapse of one or more hatch covers" that actually gave the impetus to the plunge. The Coast Guard placed the event in a more evolutionary framework. Although this difference may seem minor, it is in reality, important.

The NTSB stated that between 3:30 p.m., November 10 and the actual moment of the sinking, the decks of the FITZGERALD were awash with green water. The Coast Guard concluded the water was entering her cargo through the nonweathertight hatches. Since the sheer strake on the vessel extended 15 3/4 inches above the weather deck for the entire length of the vessel, any water reaching the deck was trapped there. As more water entered the holds and ballast tanks, her freeboard decreased, further aggravating the problem.

After completing a structural analysis of the hatch covers, the NTSB concluded that the conditions of loss of freeboard and trim as a result of flooding, could have "imposed sufficient hydrostatic loads to cause a hatch cover failure and collapse under static loading." [5]

Based on the ANDERSON'S reports, the NTSB used a significant wave height of 25 feet in its calculations. The NTSB determined that by 7:15 p.m. on November 10, enough water had entered the FITZGERALD to lower her freeboard to near zero at the Number 1 or most forward hatch. Under the condition of near zero freeboard, a 25 foot wave would produce a static head of *12.5 feet,* sufficient enough to cause a collapse of the hatch. The hatches were only designed to withstand a *4 foot* head of water.[6]

The quartering seas faced by the FITZGERALD during the storm caused a piling effect in the area aft of the forward deckhouse, which would have further increased the static head of water. Stresses caused by the dynamic forces of the boarding seas would only have added to the static stresses and accelerated the hatch cover collapse. [7]

The NTSB determined the "hatch cover failure would have been severe enough to allow rapid massive flooding of the cargo hold. Since there were no watertight bulkheads within the cargo hold, the flooding water would have progressed throughout the hold within minutes, causing the vessel to sink bow first to the bottom of the lake. Upon impact with the bottom, the midship portion disintegrated and the stern section rolled over, coming to rest upside down. [7]

As the Coast Guard investigation discovered, the lack of a method to determine if the cargo hold was flooding and pump it out if it was, only accentuated the problem by preventing the crew from taking effective action.

After a very detailed analysis, the NSTB determined that the current hatch design as used on the FITZGERALD "would have permitted significant amounts of water to enter the FITZGER-

ALD's cargo hold under the seas conditions encountered on November 10, 1975." [8]

The NTSB ruled out the possibility of the FITZGERALD breaking in two on the surface, stating that "an analysis of various flooding conditions indicated that the stress levels from longitudinal bending movements were well below that which would cause a structural failure on the surface. The proximity of the bow and stern sections on the bottom of Lake Superior indicated that the vessel sank in one piece and broke apart either when it hit bottom or as it descended. Therefore, the FITZGERALD did not sustain a massive structural failure of the hull while on the surface." [9]

The NTSB also concluded that the FITZGERALD did not capsize, determining that: "If three or less adjacent ballast tanks on the same side of the vessel were completely flooded, the FITZGERALD would not have capsized. The vessel also would not have capsized if water had entered only the cargo hold through openings between the hatch covers and the hatch openings. In each case, the roll angle would not have been sufficient to produce a cargo shift. However, under the combined effects of flooding two ballast tanks, the tunnel and the cargo hold, the FITZGERALD would have capsized within minutes. If the vessel had capsized, however, all the hatch covers would probably have been torn away by the force of the shifting taconite pellets. The underwater survey of the wreckage showed that hatch cover numbers 3 and 4 were still in place. The final position of the wreckage indicated that if the FITZGERALD had capsized, it must have suffered a structural failure before hitting the lake bottom. The bow section would have had to right itself and the stern portion would have had to capsize before coming to rest on the bottom. It is, therefore, concluded that the FITZGERALD did not capsize on the surface." [10]

The possibility of grounding was also considered by the NTSB, but dismissed due to a lack of reliable evidence. The reconstructed vessel trackline took her three miles north of the shoal; no indication of any bottom damage to the vessel was found by the CURV and finally was the fact that the NTSB had earlier concluded the FITZGERALD had suffered her reported damage prior to reaching the shoal area.[11] A complete list of the NTSB conclusions is at the end of this addendum.

Two interesting points highlighted by the NTSB Report included:

1. As determined by NTSB computer studies, the maximum vertical movement of the FITZGERALD during the height of the storm was *only five feet,* even when allowing for heave, roll and pitch.

2. An October, 1977 inspection of the ARTHUR B. HORNER, the FITZGERALD's sister-ship, revealed that light could be seen through the gasket to hatch coaming interface in 45 percent of the hatches, and in some instances, the distance between the gasket and coaming exceeded 1/2 inch. Fifteen percent of the clamps were improperly adjusted. [12]

The NTSB also made 25 recommendations to three organizations; 19 to the Coast Guard, four to the American Bureau of Shipping; and two to the National Oceanic and Atmospheric Administration. Many were a virtual repetition of those in the Coast Guard report. As of early 1981, compliance with the recommendations were mixed.

Generally, those dealing with the theoretical tightening of inspections of vessel seaworthiness were acted on, and those on the subject of design improvements were given further study.

The most positive answer to any recommendation was that concerning depth finders; the Coast Guard on July 31, 1977 (prior to the NTSB report) requiring their use on any commercial vessel 1,600 gross tons and over. [13]

In the twenty year interval since the tragic FITZGERALD loss, Coast Guard SAR capability on the Great Lakes and particularly Lake Superior has, in my opinion, generally decreased although there have been bright spots. Specifically:

The old 110-foot harbor tug NAUGATUCK was replaced in December, 1978 with the 140-foot tug KATMAI BAY. The KATMAI BAY is one of a new group of six icebreaking tugs (BRIS-

TOL BAY, MOBILE BAY, BISCAYNE BAY, NEAH BAY and MORROW BAY) introduced into the Great Lakes during the 1978-80 period as replacements for older, World War II vintage vessels. The tugs, built in Tacoma, Washington, represent the Coast Guard's minimally manned cutter concept for personnel economy. Although the KATMAI BAY's 2,500 horsepower engine provides a speed of 16 knots, a large improvement over the NAUGATUCK's 9 knots, it is not a heavy weather rescue craft. The NAUGATUCK has since been decommissioned.[15] The World War II built, 180-foot buoy tenders on the lakes will eventually be replaced by the 225-foot JUNIPER class buoy tenders. At least some of the new vessels will be built by Marinette Marine, in Marinette, Wisconsin.

The Coast Guard air capability operating from Traverse City was also upgraded, at least for a time. In October 1978 the three antiquated HU-16 Grumman Albatross aircraft were replaced by three HC-131A Convair 24D aircraft reactivated from the Air Force. The HU-16, with a speed of 140 knots, had a 10 hour flight endurance, while the old HC-131A only had an endurance of 5 1/2 hours. Two years later the HC-131As were transferred out. In the summer of 1982 Traverse City received several new HU-25 Falcon jet aircraft to permanently replace the older, slower HC-131As.[2] The HU-25s have a speed of 410 knots and a flight endurance of 4 1/2 hours. While the Falcons may appear to be an advantage, it is at best a questionable one, since one of the critical values of a SAR aircraft is the ability to go slow enough to perform an effective aerial search. With the Falcon's 410 knot speed and short endurance, it would appear ill-suited to this mission. The Falcons were later withdrawn and presently (1995) no fixed wing aircraft are stationed at Traverse City. The Coast Guard Chicago air station is also planned for a summer only operation leaving only Traverse City and Detroit (Selfridge) to cover the lakes.

In the summer of 1983 two new HH-65 Dolphin Aerospatile helicopters replaced the old HH-52A Sikorsky Sea Guards. This change was a significant upgrade in SAR assets. Flight time from Traverse City to Lake Superior decreased from 90 minutes to 60 minutes.[3] Later the HH-65s were replaced with HH-60J Jayhawks, a Coast Guard version of the rugged Army HH-60 Black-hawk. In February 1995 the smaller and less capable, HH-65s replaced the HH-60s.

Since November 1, 1980 exposure (survival) suits for Great Lakes vessels have become part of the lifesaving gear.[4] This single improvement represents an immense advance in victim survival chances, if and it is a big if, the crew receives proper training in their use.

By 1980, LORAN C (Long Range Navigation) was in Great Lakes operation, providing for greater navigational accuracy. In the early 1990s, GPS (Global Positioning System) was in common use, further increasing navigation accuracy.

While the Coast Guard juggled its surface and air assets on the Great Lakes, it decreased its manned facilities. Prior to the summer of 1982, the Coast Guard effectively closed the Grand Marais, Michigan station, reducing it from a fully manned rescue facility to one operated by volunteers of the Coast Guard Auxiliary. This very minimal level of capability was only kept as the result of strong efforts by local legislators.

The Coast Guard rationale for closing the station was based on the cold "facts" of the cost-benefit-ratio. In the years 1978 and 1979, the station performed only 10 SAR missions and since its annual operational budget was $200,000, it was obviously too expensive. By contrast, the icebreaker MACKINAW burns approximately $12,000 of fuel in a 24-hour period of serious ice-breaking (1983 dollars). This means that in 17 days, the MACK-INAW burns enough fuel to keep the Grand Marais station operating for a full year![5]

The closing of the station and the removal of her 44-foot rescue boat left a 170 mile stretch of Lake Superior coast without any viable Coast Guard protection. The nearest stations still operating are at Marquette, 60 miles to the west and Sault Ste. Marie, 80 miles to the east. It is critical to remember that the Sault station is below the Soo Locks, thus adding even more time to a SAR response. Incredibly, when questioned about the effect of closing the station, the Coast Guard stated any SAR requirement could be met with Traverse City helicopter assets (60 minute

187

flight time) or, if necessary, a trailable rescue boat is available to be brought down from Marquette Station.[6] The "rescue boat" in question is a mere Boston Whaler. A fine boat, but in comparison, more suited for sport fishing than heavy rescue.

The future of the Coast Guard on the Great Lakes is at best shaky. In January 1982 the Coast Guard announced that to help reduce a budget shortfall, three Wisconsin, three Michigan and one Minnesota SAR stations would be either closed or downgraded. Lake Superior stations included for force reduction were at Bayfield, Wisconsin; Sault Ste. Marie, Hancock and Marquette, Michigan; and the North Superior Station at Grand Marais, Minnesota. The North Superior Station was only recently reopened as a result of the FITZGERALD loss. The 290-foot, 38 year old (in 1982) icebreaker MACKINAW would also be decommissioned. Nationwide, 15 SAR stations were to be closed and eight reduced, eleven cutters decommissioned and overall the Coast Guard reduced by 3,400 personnel.

Luckily last minute political maneuvering by Great Lakes legislators managed to hold off the reductions for the immediate future. In the years following North Superior Station was reduced to only having an on call SAR detachment out of Duluth. In early 1995 it was announced that Marquette Station as well as numerous other Great Lakes stations were again being considered for inactivation. The icebreaker MACKINAW, the most capable Coast Guard vessel on the lakes, but now 50 years old, was again slated for decommissioning. Under great political pressure, the Coast Guard reluctantly agreed to keep her running for another year. By any standard, she is on her deathbed. But she will not die of old age, disease or injury, but by official neglect. She does not fit the Coast Guard model of a minimally manned vessel. Breaking ice is a function of size and brute strength, qualities the MACKINAW excels in. It isn't a finesse job. Whether its ships, stations or aircraft, the writing is clearly on the wall. Great Lakes SAR capability clearly will continue to erode.

Perhaps, the best conceptualization of the entire problem of the Coast Guard SAR capability versus vessel safety is expressed by the Lake Carriers Association when their president stated ". . . vessels navigating that (Lake Superior) or any other system should be self-sufficient to the extent practicable with an absolute minimum of federal protectionism."[7]

The NTSB was not, however, in complete agreement concerning the cause of the loss or the surrounding circumstances. The dissenting opinion, part of the NTSB report, was written by Philip A. Hogue, a member of the NTSB. An edited version follows:

"The most probable cause of the sinking of the SS EDMUND FITZGERALD in Lake Superior on 10 November, 1975, was a shoaling which first generated a list, the loss of two air vents, and a fence wire. Secondarily, within a period of 3 to 4 hours, an undetected, progressive, massive flooding of the cargo hold resulted in a total loss of buoyancy from which, diving into a wall of water, the FITZGERALD never recovered."

"The record indicates that the FITZGERALD was in all respects seaworthy prior to the commencement of her final voyage. Testimony as to the prudence and competence of her Master, Captain McSorley, is abundant. Paraphrasing the words of various witnesses, he was the best captain of the best ship in the fleet operated by the Oglebay-Norton Company. In recognition of this reputation, crew members specifically sought employment on the SS EDMUND FITZGERALD. Further, available evidence indicates that Captain McSorley would not commence a voyage into predicted bad weather without first insuring that all the hatch covers were effectively secure."

"Between the first reported damage and the time of the sinking, approximately 3 to 4 hours later, seas of 25 to 30 feet and winds gusting to 80 knots were variously observed. Without exception, expert testimony has affirmed the fact that seas in shoal waters are inherently more violent and wild than in open water. It follows, therefore, that subsequent to her initial sustained damage, the FITZGERALD suffered progressive damage from laboring, rolling, and pitching for the next 3 to 4 hours as it proceeded toward Whitefish Point Light."

"At or about 1730, Captain Woodard aboard the Swedish vessel AVAFORS received a report from Captain McSorley stating the FITZGERALD had a "bad list," had lost both radars and was taking heavy seas over the deck in one of the worst seas he had ever been in. In approximately 2 hours from the initial report of a list, the FITZGERALD had acquired a "bad list" and sustained the loss of both radars."

"Approximately 1 hour 40 minutes later at or about 1910, the FITZGERALD reported it was holding its own. This was the last transmission ever heard from the FITZGERALD. Aside from the expert testimony elicited at the Coast Guard Marine Board hearing, it is self-evident that Captain McSorley had a damaged ship, and that he did not know how damaged she was."

"Despite the difficulty experienced, in retrospect, by Captain Cooper days later before the Coast Guard Marine Board, in pinpointing the position of the FITZGERALD over various and sundry shoals, the fact remains that in his most fresh, spontaneous and free report of the accident to his company less than 24 hours after the accident, Captain Cooper variously stated, "I AM POSITIVE HE WENT OVER THAT SIX (6) FATHOM BANK!" and "I KNOW DAMN WELL HE WAS IN ON THAT THIRTY-SIX (36) FOOT SPOT, AND IF HE WAS IN THERE, HE MUST HAVE TAKEN SOME HELL OF A SEAS. I SWEAR HE WENT IN THERE. IN FACT, WE WERE TALKING ABOUT IT. WE WERE CONCERNED THAT HE WAS IN TOO CLOSE, THAT HE WAS GOING TO HIT THAT SHOAL OFF CARIBOU, I MEAN, GOD, HE WAS ABOUT THREE MILES OFF THE LAND BEACON.""

"It is reasonable to assume, from all that is known of Captain McSorley, that his first report of damage was based on damage sustained immediately prior to 1530 and that it was no small consideration that caused Captain McSorley to ask the ANDERSON to stay with him, saying, "I will check down so that you can close the distance between us.""

"In order for me to concur with the Safety Board's majority, I have to assume that the true positions and tracklines of the FITZGERALD were those that would have been pursued in normal weather and that she remained well clear of shallow water and shoals. "

"I strongly doubt that was the case because Captain Cooper and Captain Pulcer, the former Master of the FITZGERALD, both testified that despite the general use of traffic lanes on Lake Superior, heavy weather contributed to the selection of ship courses. Indeed, on the day of the sinking, Captain Cooper of the ANDERSON originally intended to clear Michipicoten about 2 to 2 1/2 miles off. Nonetheless, due to weather, he finally cleared Michipicoten West End Light by 7.7 miles. Thereafter, he steered a number of courses ranging from 125 degrees to 141 degrees. All factors considered, it is my assumption that the

FITZGERALD was variously steering various courses and for approximately the same reasons. In fact, if the FITZGERALD had also been 7.7 miles off Michipicoten, instead of 2.2 miles as estimated or recollected, and steering 141 degrees, she certainly would have been in the shoal waters Captain Cooper reported to his company."

"Considering the fact that no testimony has ever been produced to show that the FITZGERALD had ever arrived in port without dry cargo and the overall success of the hatch covers generally in use on the Great Lakes for many years, I have great difficulty accepting the argument that one or more of the hatches on the FITZGERALD on the day of the accident were either nonwatertight or that they failed prior to the first report of damage. If, in fact, hatch failure or loss of weathertight integrity occurred prior to the FITZGERALD's sinking I can only surmise that such failure or failures occurred subsequent to the first list reported on or about 1530 and prior to the sinking on or about 1910."

"I place great credence in Captain Cooper's testimony that the FITZGERALD was in proximity or over shoal waters; first, because his judgment is the most expert to be found at the scene and as much as anything else, the FITZGERALD reported her first casualties at that almost exact time. I could have doubts of one fact or another, but putting two and two together plus the subsequent events, I am strongly convinced that the FITZGERALD received her first damage as I have indicated and that from that time until the sinking, the FITZGERALD's condition deteriorated beyond the Captain's knowledge and beyond recovery."

"Naval Architect Richard A. Stearn, on p. 1227 of the Marine Board of Investigation stated, "If there was a list, it must have been — if it was any substantial amount of list, it must have been from a fracture in the hull caused by grounding or other means.""

"Captain Cooper on pp. 565 and 566 of the Marine Board of Investigation Report stated. "I believe that she was cracked somewhere. She was taking water fast enough because what he told me was that, 'I have a list and I am taking water' and I said, 'Have you got your pumps on?' and he said, 'Both of them.' ""

"On p. 2140, Captain Cooper stated, "I have never known a ship to lose a fence rail in a seaway." On pp. 2152 and 2153, Captain Cooper stated again, "The only solution I can have to a fence rail breaking is —

you can't break one by sagging a ship, but you would have to bend the ship, hog it up in the middle, to put such a tension on the fence rail that you would break it. That is five-eighths wire rope with three strands running in through there. You might break one, but you can't conceivably think of breaking three."

"On p. 2490, Captain Delmore Webster states, "I think he set over on one of those shoals and that was the moment that his fence rail broke.""

"All of the foregoing expert testimony strongly supports the conclusion that the initial list and loss of fence railing were induced by shoaling."

"On p. 1962, Captain Woodard, the pilot on the Swedish vessel AVAFORS stated, "It was one of the biggest and wildest seas I have ever been in, I mean fast." On p. 1963, he said, "The sea was straight up and down and a lot of them were coming at you. It was not like big rollers.""

"Without exception, vessels in the vicinity of the FITZGERALD's sinking absolutely refused to consider turning around in such severe wind and sea conditions."

"After studying all available information, it is my firm conclusion that the FITZGERALD shoaled and sustained her initial damage shortly before 1530 and that thereafter, the various workings of the vessel and loss of watertight integrity led to her sudden and totally unexpected sinking."

/s/ PHILIP ALLISON HOGUE
Member[22]

In defense of the NTSB report, James B. King, the NTSB Chairman, wrote a rebuttal to Mr. Hogue's contentions. An edited version follows:

"I agree fully with the report adopted by the majority, but because of the importance of the accident and the controversy it has engendered, I believe it worthwhile to address in some detail the contentions which the dissent raises. The dissent offers eight contentions to support its version of the probable cause, and this opinion will discuss each in turn."

"The first contention, upon which the dissent principally rests, is that Captain Cooper of the ANDERSON stated after the accident that he believed that the FITZGERALD had grounded north of Caribou Island. This statement: (1) was contradicted by Captain Cooper himself under circumstances more likely to elicit a correct recollection and (2) is inconsistent with the independent navigational evidence. The statement upon which the dissent relies was not made under oath, was made without benefit of charts, with no other witnesses present, and without crossexamination. When Captain Cooper had an opportunity to testify before the Marine Board and to refer to navigational charts, he contradicted his statement concerning a grounding, and charted a trackline for the FITZGERALD which corresponds to the trackline presented in the report."

"At the Marine Board Captain Cooper and Chief Mate Clark both testified that the FITZGERALD was not near the shoal area. Captain Cooper testified that at 1540 the FITZGERALD was in the position the ANDERSON reached when she changed course to 141° T. This position is well clear of the shoal. Chief Mate Clark testified that when the ANDERSON changed course to 141° F the FITZGERALD was right on their heading flasher and "Maybe he didn't go in there (close to Caribou Island)."

"Moreover, the "grounding" statement is inconsistent with the independent navigational evidence. First, the "6-fathom spot" to which Captain Cooper referred to is noted in lake Survey Chart No. 9 but was later determined by hydrographic survey not to exist. Second, the FITZGERALD could not have passed over the "6-fathom spot" on a course of 141° T without coming and remaining hard aground just north of Caribou Island in less than 4 fathoms of water. Moreover, it would have been physically impossible for the FITZGERALD to travel from her 1520 position obtained by the ANDERSON to a position in which grounding would have been possible by 1530. Such a journey would have required that the FITZGERALD proceed through mountainous seas at a speed greater than her top speed, nor is there any evidence of grounding in the approximately 270 ft of exposed bottom plating on the FITZGERALD stern."

"The dissent's second contention is that Captain McSorley's report of a list and vents and fence rail down occurred when the FITZGERALD was in the shoal area, and indicates that the FITZGERALD had grounded. As mentioned above, the probable trackline shows that the FITZGERALD was not near a shoal area. In any event, a grounding could not have caused loss of the two vents. The two vents are massive, and a heavy impact above the deck level would have been required. The reported list, which the dissent takes to indicate grounding at that moment, could not have developed instantaneously. Whatever event caused the list had to have occurred sometime before 1520."

"The dissent's third contention, closely parallel to that just discussed, is that loss of the fence rail must have been caused by hogging. As discussed above, impact by a heavy object would have been required to knock down the vents. The object which knocked down the vents could also easily have knocked down the fence rails. Thus, although hogging could have caused loss of the fence rail, it could not have caused loss of the vents. On the other hand, impact by a heavy object could have caused the loss of both."

"As a fourth contention, the dissent cites the testimony of Mr. Stearn and Captain Webster. These two opinions, of course, are speculations of persons who were not near the FITZGERALD at the time of the casualty. As mentioned previously, these opinions are inconsistent with the navigational evidence."

"The fifth contention is that because Captain McSorley was a competent master he would have insured that all hatch covers were secured. Captain McSorley's competence was unquestioned, but investigations have disclosed that a number of competent Great Lakes bulk cargo vessels do not maintain weathertight hatches. During the lay-up period of 1976-1977 the Coast Guard conducted an extensive program of hatch cover inspections to insure that the clamps were properly adjusted and that the hatches were weathertight. The hatch clamps were frequently adjusted while the Coast Guard inspector was still aboard to show that the hatch covers would pass a hose test for weather tightness. Many times the hatch clamps were tightened to the point of failure without achieving the weathertightness of the closure. Furthermore, even after this extensive program, Safety Board investigators found loose clamps and nonweathertight hatch covers on Great Lakes bulk cargo vessels during the fall of 1977."

"Calculations indicate that each of the 68 clamps on FITZGERALD's hatch covers must apply about 2,400 pounds at force to insure a tight seal from the gasket. Furthermore, Great Lake masters believe the weight of the hatch cover alone, about 14,000 pounds, would make the hatch cover weathertight. Calculations indicate more than 178,000 pounds is required."

"A sixth contention, also concerning hatch covers, is that there is not testimony to insure that the FITZGERALD ever arrived in port without dry cargo. Although there is no testimony concerning wet cargo, 26,116 tons of taconite could absorb 4 to 6.7 percent water by weight (1044 to 1750 tons) without any free water being seen in the cargo hold. On occasions Great Lakes bulk cargo vessels have arrived in port with 2 to 4 inches of water in the cargo hold."

"The dissent also argues that the tracklines of the ANDERSON and the FITZGERALD and their relative positions could not be reconstructed as stated in the Coast Guard Report. After extensive analysis of the testimony, the tracklines in the report of the vessel were reconstructed using logged times and positions. Although the data used were not of the "navigation textbook quality" the testimony does match the reconstructed tracklines if some times are adjusted. By calculating courses and speeds from positions "logged as normal course of business" the errors of time are evident."

"The difference in relative bearing as observed by the ANDERSON's master and mate can be explained by the fact that the two hearings were taken 20 minutes apart. Furthermore, the motion of the FITZGERALD relative to the ANDERSON, on courses 141° T, respectively, would have caused the bearings to drift right."

"The dissent's final contention is that the FITZGERALD was steering various courses between Michipicoten Island and Caribou Island between 1359 and 1520. The standard usually accepted trackline for this route is 141° T. Great Lakes vessels depart from the recommended tracklines to take advantage of the lee provided by shore as did the ANDERSON and the FITZGERALD. The ANDERSON changed her course to 230° T while north of Michipicoten Island to allow for a predicted wind shift to the northwest and to allow herself more searoom from a lee shore. At the time of this wind shift the FITZGERALD was south of Michipicoten Island and had no reason to alter course from the accepted track of 141° T. Any course change the FITZGERALD would have made to reduce the rolling of the vessel would have been to the east. A course change to a course more southerly than 141° T would have produced more pronounced rolling and would have been unacceptable to the master."

"I have reviewed the dissent carefully and given careful consideration to Member Hogue's opinions, but I am unable to find the evidence in the testimony or reports which would permit me to join him."

/s/ JAMES B. KING
Chairman[23]

NTSB CONCLUSIONS

1. The FITZGERALD's hatch covers were not weathertight and allowed water to enter the cargo hold over an extended period. This water was not detected because it migrated down through the cargo. There was no method provided for sounding the cargo other than visual observations, nor was there any method for dewatering the cargo hold with the vessel trimmed by the bow.

2. Amendments to the Great Lakes Load Line Regulations in 1969, 1971, and 1973 allow Great Lakes bulk carriers to load deeper. This deeper loading increased deck wetness which caused an increase in the flooding rate through nonweathertight hatches or other nonweathertight openings.

3. The topside vents and fence rail were damaged before 1520 either by a heavy object coming adrift on deck or by a floating object coming aboard with the seas. The FITZGERALD's hull plating probably was damaged also; the damage propagated and caused flooding of the ballast tanks and tunnel.

4. Flooding of ballast tanks and the tunnel caused trim and a list. Detection of ballast tank flooding prompted the ballast pumps to be started. However, the flooding rate through the hull damage, which was propagating, increased and exceeded the capacity of the pumping system.

5. The hull stress levels, even with a substantial amount of flooding, were low enough that the hull girder did not fail before the sinking.

6. The forces on the hatch covers caused by boarding seas were sufficient to cause damage and collapse. These forces increased as flooding caused a list and reduced the vessel's freeboard.

7. Flooding of the cargo hold caused by one or more collapsed hatch covers was massive and progressed throughout the hold. Flooding was so rapid that the vessel sank before the crew could transmit a distress call.

8. The vessel either plunged or partially capsized and plunged under the surface. The hull failed either as the vessel sank or when the bow struck the bottom.

9. The availability of a fathometer aboard the FITZGERALD would have provided additional navigational data and would have required less dependence on the ANDERSON for navigational assistance.

10. The most probable trackline of the FITZGERALD, from west of Michipicoten Island to the position of her wreckage, lies east of the shoal areas north and east of Caribou Island; therefore, damage from grounding would have been unlikely.

11. The shoal area north of Caribou Island is not shown in sufficient detail on Lake Survey Chart No. 9 to indicate the extent of this hazard to navigation. A contour presentation of this hazard would allow mariners to better assess this area and would help to eliminate the erroneous conclusion that there are isolated spots of shallow water, where in fact there is a large area of shoal water less than 10 fathoms deep.

12. Insufficient water depth has been observed at some loading and discharge piers. "Groundings" of vessels at these locations induce hull stresses of unknown magnitudes and create the potential of undetected hull damage and wear.

13. Although the National Weather Service accurately predicted the direction and velocity of the wind expected over the eastern end of Lake Superior on November 10, 1975, the predicted wave heights were significantly less than those observed.

14. Loading information on the FITZGERALD and other Great Lakes bulk cargo vessels was not adequate.

15. Great Lakes bulk cargo vessels normally can avoid severe storms. The limiting sea state for Great Lakes bulk cargo vessels should be determined, and the operation of vessels in sea states above this limiting value should be restricted.

197

16. The presence of an EPIRB aboard the FITZGERALD would have provided immediate automatic transmission of an emergency signal which would have allowed search units to locate the position of the accident. The accurate location of this position would have reduced the extent of the search area.

17. Installation of trim and list indicating instruments on the FITZGERALD would have provided the master an early indication of flooding that would have an adverse effect on the vessel. These instruments would have given an indication of whether the master's corrective action was adequate.

18. The surface search and rescue capability of the Coast Guard on November 10 was inadequate. [24]

1. Correspondence, National Transportation Safety Board, December 1, 1977.

2. MARINE CASUALTY REPORT, S.S. EDMUND FITZGERALD; sinking in Lake Superior, November 10, 1975. NATIONAL TRANSPORTATION SAFETY BOARD, Report Number NTSB-MAR-78-3.

3. MARINE CASUALTY REPORT, S.S. EDMUND FITZGERALD; sinking in Lake Superior, November 10, 1975 with loss of life; U.S. COAST GUARD MARINE BOARD OF INVES-TIGATION REPORT AND COMMANDANT'S ACTION, Report Number USCG 16732/64216, Department of Transportation, Coast Guard, P. 92.

4. NTSB REPORT, p. 36.

5. Ibid, p. 25.

6. Ibid, p. 25.

7. Ibid, p. 26.

8. Ibid, p. 27.

9. Ibid, p. 27

10. Ibid, p. 28.

11. Ibid, p. 29.

12. Correspondence, National Transportation Safety Board. September 15, 1978.

1 3. Correspondence, National Transportation Safety Board. December 31,1980.

14. DETROIT MARINE HISTORIAN, JOURNAL OF THE MARINE HISTORICAL SOCI-ETY OF DETROIT (November 1980).

15. LAKE LOG CHIPS. (April 17, 1979, November 27, 1980), Center for Archival Collections, Bowling Green State University, Bowling Green, Ohio.

16. Memorandum, United States Coast Guard, November 26, 1980. THE COAST GUARD, ITS MISSIONS AND OBJECTIVES, Department of Transportation, p. 67.

17. Ibid.

18. Memorandum, United States Coast Guard, December 15,1980.

19. MARQUETTE MINING JOURNAL. Marquette, Michigan. September 3, 30; October 8, 22; November 7, 1980. Correspondence. Senator Donald W. Riegle, Jr. to Commandant, U.S.C.G., September 4, 1980.

Correspondence. Commander, Ninth Coast Guard District to Representative Robert W. David, November 3, 1980.

20. Ibid.

21. Correspondence, Lake Carriers' Association, November 6, 1980.

22. NTSB REPORT, pp. 44 - 48.

23. NTSB REPORT, pp. 41 - 43.

24. NTSB REPORT, pp. 34 - 35.

THE LEGEND LIVES ON

There is something very special about the EDMUND FITZGERALD. It just will not fade from the public mind.

For many people, the FITZGERALD has become part of the legend of the Great Lakes, passing from fact into the nether world of fable. There are those who do not realize that the FITZGER-ALD was a real ship, crewed by living, breathing men and not simply a creation of songwriter Gordon Lightfoot.

The FITZGERALD has also become a cottage industry. Consumers can buy books, T-shirts, sweat shirts, posters, prints, videos, coffee cups, post cards, mugs, baseball caps, jewelry and all manner of flotsam commemorating the vessel's loss. There is also a theatrical production called "Ten November." If the result of all this memorabilia is to remember the tragic loss of the "good ship and crew" and to gain a better appreciation for the Lakes, it is all to the good. If however, it is simply a crass commercialization of a terrible disaster, it speaks poorly of our values.

UPDATE

The most distinctive annual memorial ceremony for the FITZGERALD is that conducted at Detroit's Mariners' Church. The special service had its beginning the day after the wreck when the rector, Reverend Richard W. Ingalls, tolled the church bell 29 times, once for each member of the lost crew. Afterwards he went to the sanctuary and remembered them in prayer. The news media picked up his actions and widely reported the solemn recognition of the tragedy. Canadian folk singer Gordon Lightfoot read one of the accounts and built it into the ballad "The Wreck of the EDMUND FITZGERALD." The annual service, held the nearest Sunday to November 10, memorializes the FITZGERALD as well as all Great Lakes Shipwrecks. The

Mariners' Church was founded in 1842 when Julia Anderson, the widow of an early Detroit military commander, bequeathed land and money to construct a church for seamen.

Captain Jesse B. Cooper, the ex-master of the ARTHUR M. ANDERSON, died on April 6, 1993. A veteran of 44 years of Lake navigation, he received the Coast Guard Distinguished Public Service Award for his efforts following the FITZGERALD loss.

In July 1993 one of the FITZGERALD's old anchors was recovered from the Detroit River west of Belle Isle by the Great Lakes Maritime Institute (GLMI) as a fund raising project. The FITZGERALD had anchored behind the island in January 1974 but when she attempted to haul the anchor, it snagged on ice and was lost. It remained lost until GLMI divers located it after an extensive search. The anchor weighed six tons and stood 12 feet high. Today the anchor stands at the Dossin Great Lakes Museum as a memorial to the FITZGERALD.

FITZGERALD has also been the subject of numerous expeditions, each reexamining the wreckage in an attempt to discover new information on the mysterious case.

CALYPSO - 1980

On September 24, 1980, divers from Jacques Cousteau's CALYPSO, Albert Falco and Colin Mounier, used their two man submarine to explore the FITZGERALD. This was the first manned submersible to visit the wreck. The CALYPSO was in the Great Lakes as part of a film project on the Saint Lawrence River. Jacques was not aboard the CALYPSO with the exception of a brief visit to Detroit to accept the key to city when the vessel passed upbound. The trip was under the operational leadership of his son, Jean-Michel.

The trip to the Lakes was under the sponsorship of the Cousteau Society and the National Film Board of Canada. Its purpose was to observe marine life, document pollution and trace the route of the early French explorers, missionaries and trappers. The ultimate product was to be a film focusing on the Saint Lawrence River and its tributaries.

Tragedy struck the expedition on September 3, 1980 when one of their men was killed while diving in Lake Ontario. The cause of death was an apparent air embolism. It was the first diving death in 30 years of CALYPSO's operations and it badly shook the crew.

After spending approximately 30 minutes below, an extremely brief period, the Cousteau team determined that the FITZGERALD broke in two on the surface and did not sink quickly. Jean-Michel stated the two divers discovered, "The bow section extremely dented, something had to bang against it." They thought the damage was caused by the bow striking the stern in the heavy waves and believed the damage could not have taken place underwater. Jean-Michel stated, "It is more likely it was floating for a while and (the two broken sections) then sank together. Had the ship broken in two pieces and instantly sunk, the bow would have been further from the aft section."

The final Cousteau film on the Saint Lawrence contained only a very brief section on the FITZGERALD

ROV - 1989

To further evidence the high public interest in the FITZGERALD, from August 22-25, 1989, the wreck was explored using state of the art Remote Operated Vehicle (ROV) technology. The expedition was organized by Michigan Sea Grant and included experts from Deep Diving Systems of Falmouth, Massachusetts, U.S. Fish and Wildlife Service, National Geographic Society, WQED-TV (Pittsburgh), WJRT-TV (Flint), Great Lakes Shipwreck Historical Society, National Oceanographic and Atmospheric Administration, U.S. Army Corps of Engineers, Michigan Department of Natural Resources, State Historical Society of Wisconsin, Royal Ontario Museum, Ontario Marine Heritage Conservation Program and marine historians and archaeologists from the United States and Canada. The Fish and Wildlife Service's R.V. GRAYLING served as the mother ship.

The 1989 expedition provided the first realistic field test of a new towed survey system (TSS) developed by Deep Diving Systems. The TSS included an ROV, three dimensional (3-D) imagery system and sled. The ROV was self-propelled, free

The RV GRAYLING on station over the FITZGERALD. Author

swimming and tethered (to the sled) allowing unique flexibility in exploring the wreck. Equipped with lights, miniature stereo-scopic color cameras and wide angle lenses, it provided unparalleled video imagery. Format shot was 1/2 inch Beta. The sled was equipped with high resolution scanning sonar, a separate underwater video camera, lights, a heading transponder and acoustic

Lowering the TSS over the stern of the GRAYLING. Photo by Don Shomette

The concrete block is part of the GRAYLING mooring system. The film crew is from National Geographic. The TSS is in the foreground.

navigation pinger/transponder. It was the "garage" for the tethered ROV.

After the sled was positioned, the ROV deployed out of the sled on the tether cable and commenced exploration. In the ROV control room on the GRAYLING a pilot flew the free swimming device. Extreme skill was required to keep the ROV cable free of entangling wreckage and still achieve the necessary video documentation. The digital scanning sonar and pinger/transponder enabled the pilot to constantly track the relative positions of the sled and ROV.

While the FITZGERALD was undoubtedly the highlight of the project, the overall scope included a number of other objectives:

1. Completion of 3-dimensional ROV surveys on selected deep water shipwreck sites near Whitefish Point (FITZGERALD) and Rogers City, Michigan (F.T. BARNEY).

2. Test the capabilities of ROV and underwater positioning systems technology for future shipwreck surveys within Michigan's Great Lakes in accordance with State of Michigan historic preservation guidelines and recommendations of the

The bow of the FITZGERALD as recorded on the GRAYLING down scanner.   Photo by Author

federal Abandoned Shipwreck Act of 1987. Also to assess the effectiveness of this technology for survey, assessment and management of coastal zone and underwater cultural resources.

3. Focus regional-national media attention on Michigan's shipwreck resources and the value of these resources for tourism, recreation, historic preservation and archeology.

4. Provide an opportunity for professionals engaged in shipwreck and natural resources management programs to exchange ideas and skills, in the hope of stimulating further research.

The objectives were clearly achieved, especially that relating to the media. National and world-wide attention was focussed on the FITZGERALD. On-site interviews were conducted by National Public Radio, Good Morning America and Late Night America. News items were carried by all the major networks and news stories ran throughout the midwest as well as nationally. A telephone interview was even given to a New Zealand news agency!

The FITZGERALD video tape was used to further public understanding of the tragedy. The Great Lakes Shipwreck Historical Society used part of it in a documentary on the vessel while National Geographic Society Explorer used a segment in a broadcast program.

Author with TSS.   Photo by Author

This writer was privileged to be aboard GRAYLING when the ROV initially viewed the FITZGERALD. It was an event that had to be experienced to be fully understood. When the first flickering images of the long dead vessel appeared on the monitor, all conversation stopped cold. A silence every bit as deep as that surrounding the sunken steamer engulfed us. It seemed that even the activity of breathing was suspended. Eagerly we watched as the ROV moved carefully over the wreck. First the mast came into view. Then the top of the pilot house. The RDF loops were bent back a full 90 degrees, clear evidence of the force of her downward plunge. Visibility was excellent, perhaps as great as 25 feet. Ghostly images of the wreck continued to dance across the screen. When the ROV poked its nose into the pilothouse windows we collectively held our breath, but nothing other than wreckage was visible. The overhead had partially collapsed to the deck and the water cooler was knocked forward as was the radar console. Spiral microphone cables had stretched out twice their length from what was originally shown in the 1976 Coast Guard photographs.

As the ROV moved around the pilothouse, it revealed a pane of glass still intact in the stern of the charthouse. The starboard door was also open, a point not discovered in the original Coast Guard investigation. Careful examination showed that the hinges and door knob were intact and undamaged. The dogs were also vertical and not horizontal. From the undamaged condition of the door it was evident that it was not blown open by air pressure or a surge of water when the steamer dove for the bottom. Rather, it was clearly open when she sank, suggesting the tantalizing possibility that one or more members of the crew knew she was going down and made a last ditch effort to save himself.

For those few aboard the GRAYLING when the ROV made its initial survey, it was indeed a time of high drama. The silence on board GRAYLING was deafening. It seemed that even the activity of breathing was suspended.

The video taken by the ROV was immeasurably better than the grainy, black and white images the Coast Guard investigation team had to work with 13 years before. The 3-D aspects of the new technology also provided unique opportunities to discern damage not previously seen.

Although the video was shot as a means of testing the technology and gathering material for documentary purposes, rather than as a full fledged reinvestigation of the wreck, it was felt that the opportunity should be taken to have a panel of experts view the tape to see if any conclusions concerning the loss could be drawn or new evidence discovered. The tape was not intended to provide a thorough, systematic survey and only covered selected parts of the FITZGERALD.

On March 23, 1990, the volunteer panel, consisting of naval architects, marine engineers, experienced lake masters, marine historians and a marine surveyor, reviewed the more than five hours of tape. This writer served as the moderator. After the original Coast Guard investigation, this was the most concentrated effort to examine the evidence. The panel members viewed the tape during a very concentrated session and were asked to respond to the major question:

- What does the video tell us about the FITZ-GERALD, regarding cause of loss or the wrecking process?

They were asked not to argue for or against any particular theory of loss or wrecking process, but rather to relate what they were seeing in the video tape either to existing theories or to any potential new theory.

It has been said that an elephant is a mouse designed to military specifications and a camel a horse designed by a committee. With this in mind, it is easy to understand that reaching conclusions acceptable to all committee members was difficult and that the ensuing results are therefore less than startling. To help understand the panel conclusions I have added my comments in bold. The conclusions expressed are the points on which panel members unanimously agreed. They do not necessarily represent the views of any individual or organization.

CONCLUSIONS REFERENT TO WRECKING ACTION AND PROCESS.

1. There was not sufficient information from the video to determine cause of loss. **Clues, clues, clues, no answers!**
2. The port side pilothouse door is not dogged, but is open. **All doors should have been dogged during the storm. The open door suggests an attempt to leave and if not actually made, at least contemplated.**
3. The bow damage is extensive. **Video suggests it was caused by water drag during the plunge to the bottom and that the vessel struck bow first.**
4. The overall damage on the bow was not caused by surface action. **Wave action would not cause such damage. As dramatic as the destruction is, it wasn't caused by the storm.**
5. There is aftward deflection of deck gear. **This was the result of high drag on the way down.**
6. There is compression and buckling of bulwarks and main deck area forward. **This was caused by the severe impact of striking the bottom.**
7. The finding of the hatch crane is significant, but relative position would be helpful to know. The crane was not located relative to other wreckage. **It was unclear where it was carried on the steamer, aft, center or forward, thus its location on the bottom could not be placed in context.**

8. The intensity and extend of taconite coverage on the site is significant (including on top of the wreckage and particularly on the starboard side of the forward section). **The taconite resulted from the stern floating for a short period and spilling cargo on top of the forward section, verifying that the bow struck bottom first. The two sections did not sink simultaneously.**

9. The spar deck and the debris field between bow and stern were not video taped well. **Remember that the tape was shot for documentary film purposes and as a technology demonstrator, not as a pure investigation vehicle.**

MACINNIS EXPEDITION - 1994

During July 3-5, 1994 the FITZGERALD was examined by a team headed up by Canadian underwater explorer Dr. Joe MacInnis. A medical doctor with a specialty of evaluating human performance in high stress environments, he has extensive experience in ocean exploration. Twice he led groups to survey and photograph the wreck of the RMS TITANIC, as well as authored several books on underwater exploration.

During the summer of 1994 MacInnis organized and led "Great Lakes 94", a six week environmental survey of the Great Lakes and Saint Lawrence River. Projects included studying the effects of pollution, especially persistent toxins, and their entry into the food chain. Teams of U.S. and Canadian scientists from seven universities and the U.S. Environmental Protection Agency participated in the important research.

MacInnis stated the FITZGERALD work was added because, "we're hoping public interest in the FITZGERALD carries over to a broader appreciation of the health of the Great Lakes basin, which is home to 40 million people. Frankly, people are not terribly interested in toxic chemicals, but they are certainly fascinated with the FITZGERALD. And shipwrecks are a wonderful human symbol. When you dive 535 feet down and see a shipwreck torn in half, you are aware of the fact that these Lakes are powerful and special." The wreck also served as a technology demonstrator for the sonar used to locate her, the special high resolution cameras and the underwater mercury vapor lights.

209

The mother ship for the expedition was the 168-foot R.V. EDWIN LINK, owned and operated by the Harbor Branch Oceanographic Institution of Fort Pierce, Florida. The 22-foot, three man research submarine CELIA provided the diving support. A total of six dives were made over the three day period. Ten hours of video tape were shot, some of which will be used in a MacInnis produced TV documentary on the Great Lakes ecosystem.

Participating in the FITZGERALD survey was Thomas Farnquist, Executive Director of the Great Lakes Shipwreck Historical Society. Long a student of the wreck and a leader of the 1989 ROV expedition, Farnquist was particularly well qualified to examine the wreckage and comment on the CELIA's observations. Other than the short Cousteau look in 1980, this was the first time a human had "eye balled" the FITZGERALD since the day she sank, 19 years before.

In spite of three days of hard diving, the riddle of the FITZGERALD's sinking wasn't answered. Farnquist did note from the survey observations, that it was virtually impossible that the steamer broke in two on the surface (as claimed by the CALYPSO divers 14 years before). Structural damage also is more extensive than observed in earlier surveys. Farnquist commented, "It sank with incredible force, propelled downward by a monster wave and momentum from its 7,500 horsepower engines and the forward surge of 26,116 tons of taconite ore. I think it drove itself into the bottom with the screw still going and literally exploded. Conceivably, the nose of the 729-foot vessel struck bottom while the rear third was above the water's surface, as it was only 530 feet deep." Considering the devastation on the lake bottom, Farnquist further stated, "We may not know why it sank, but we know more about what happened during the sinking than we did before."

Great Lakes Shipwreck Historical Society board member Jene Quiren commented on the extensive damage to the lake bottom. The ship broke in half and dug up huge chunks of clay as it slammed into the bottom. "It really looked like a moonscape in a lot of places because the chunks of clay were so jagged and angular and really untouched after the impact." The bow plowed a 30-

foot deep trench into the glacial mud in a catastrophic collision with the lake floor. Taconite pellets were scattered for hundreds of feet around the debris and mud. The fact that they are still visible after nearly 20 years and the sharp edges of the mud ridges are cold evidence of the lack of a bottom current.

One new item discovered by the CELIA was that the stern lies roughly parallel to the bow. The original Coast Guard sketches placed it at a greater angle. They also noted extensive hull separation from the spar deck forward. The pilothouse telegraph was also observed to appear to be set at full ahead and not checked down, giving credence to the theory that she was going full ahead when she plunged. A large amount of debris was also piled against the aft pilothouse bulkhead, also indicating strong forward momentum. Not previously seen, the 90 degree bend in the stem post, indicative of the enormous force of the bottom impact. CELIA found no evidence of the crew. MacInnis stated, "The crew had no idea what happened, it was so sudden, so explosive."

Farnquist later said the video tape taken during the exploration will be used by team of marine engineers and naval architects to try to shed more light on the cause of the disaster. The same evidence review process was very effective for the 1989 survey.

SHANNON EXPEDITION - 1994

Frederick J. Shannon, a Mount Morris, Michigan businessman, conducted a privately funded survey of the FITZGERALD on July 25 - 27, 1994. The surface support ship was the Purvis Marine tug ANGLIAN LADY of Sault Ste. Marie, Ontario, the most powerful Canadian tug in the Great Lakes. The submarine used was DELTA, a 16-foot research craft owned by Delta Oceanographic of Channel Islands, California. DELTA was fully equipped with still and video cameras as well as a wide range of underwater navigation devices.

Shannon actively researched the FITZGERALD since 1983 and is a frequent lecturer on the tragedy. Armed with new information, including documents he discovered in the National Archives, as well as extensive interviews with prior FITZGERALD crewmen and marine experts, he believed his expedition would succeed in discovering the cause of loss where pervious

Canadian tug ANGLIAN LADY served as the surface support vessl for "Expedition 94."   Photo by Jeff S. Dale, "Expedition 94 LTD"

ones failed. Shannon also intended to use the results of the survey to produce a video documentary as well as a book.

This writer did review a portion of the Shannon expedition video tape. The quality is excellent and it explicitly shows the devastation of the FITZGERALD. The battered pilothouse and bow, shattered windows, torn and ripped steel, all stand in mute testimony to the greatest Lakes disaster of modern times. The open pilothouse door speaks silently but profoundly and forcefully of what might have happened.

During the fourth dive of the expedition, on Tuesday, July 26, Shannon's group discovered what they assumed to be the remains of one of the FITZGERALD's crew, something none of the previous expeditions had accomplished. Aboard Delta were the pilot, Chris Ijames, Jack Purvis and his 12 year old son Scott. The body, believed to be wearing the remains of a life jacket, was found lying on the lake bottom near the bow. Although the canvas had largely deteriorated, what is thought to be six rectangular cork blocks were clearly visible. The remains were located by accident and no special effort was made to find them. It is commonly believed the majority of the crew are still entombed in the stern.

Since the wreck is generally assumed to be in Canadian waters, the appropriate government authorities were immediately notified, as required under the expedition's dive permit. After due consideration, Dr. James Young, the Chief Coroner for Ontario, stated that "we consider that area to be a natural grave site." The deputy coroner stated that "there is no practical way to retrieve it. It's one thing to photograph it, but it's difficult to actually recover it." No effort to retrieve the remains would be made. The Canadian government continued to ensure that the wreck would be treated with respect.

The discovery of the body upset many of the surviving family members of FITZGERALD crewmen. After nearly 20 years they had largely put the terrible event behind them. Finding a body only brought the old hurt back to the surface. Many people, both private citizens and relatives, expressed concern that the various expeditions were callously exploiting the wreck site. At this writing photography of the remains has not been released.

On the seventh and final dive, Shannon left a memorial plaque just aft of the FITZGERALD's pilothouse. Inscribed in the plaque were the names of all 29 of the ill-fated crew, as well as that of the late Captain Jesse Cooper, the master of the ARTHUR M. ANDERSON, and expedition participants.

The crew of "Expedition 94" pose with the memorial plaque.
Frederick J. Shannon is holding the plaque. Photo by Jeff S. Dale,
"Expedition 94 LTD"

Looking into the pilothouse of the FITZGERALD. The engineroom telegraph is barely visible in the background. Photo by Frederick J. Shannon, "Expedition 94"

After three days of dive operations, the in-hand result was 32 hours of video tape and nearly eight hundred still photographs. After examining the newly gathered evidence closely, in November 1994 Shannon announced, "All former theories are shot; they can go back in the closet. Videos and stills we took from our submersible indicate massive structural failure. The wreckage is scattered over two acres. It could have happened on the surface, or as the boat was going down, or on impact with the bottom. However, my research suggests the boat was over used and hadn't been in up-to-par condition for over a year. It made 748 career trips in its 17 years of service, carrying over 19 million tons of cargo. That's a lot and severely strains the boat's components."

Carefully sifting through his mountainous data, Shannon concluded:

A. The FITZGERALD did not plunge to the bottom in one piece, with the propeller driving the vessel into the mud and subsequently break on impact.

B. The FITZGERALD did not "explode" during the wrecking process as suggested by earlier surveys.

C. The FITZGERALD broke up on the surface.

D. The FITZGERALD may not be in Canadian waters. Global Positioning System (GPS) readings taken on site, cast doubt on whether it is in Canada, the U.S. or right on the line, with perhaps the bow section in the U.S. and the stern in Canada.

While all of Shannon's conclusions represent significant departures from conventional theory, he is confident of their accuracy.

The pilothouse of the FITZGERALD with the open portside chartroom door.   Photo by Frederick J. Shannon, "Expedition 94"

Some Thoughts

Even without a full examination of all of the 1994 data, with the exception of the CALYPSO effort of 1980, each subsequent expedition has significantly added to our knowledge of the FITZGERALD.

- The 1989 ROV survey first discovered the open pilothouse door, establishing the potential for an effort to leave her, as well as determined the damage and deflection as caused by drag through the water while plunging for the bottom and "proved" the hull sank after the bow as evidenced by the spilled taconite.

- The MacInnis survey found more extensive hull/deck damage than previously seen and added significantly to the knowledge of the dynamics of the wrecking process. The publicity generated will continue to focus attention on the Great Lakes.

• The Shannon expedition, by finding the body in the life jacket could potentially have closed the loop in terms of crew knowledge of impending disaster. It could be suggested that at least one man knew the FITZGERALD was going to the bottom. In addition, it continued to document extensive damage to the vessel and advanced significant new theories as to the cause and process of wrecking.

Although perhaps a bit morbid, I believe it is worthwhile to speculate on the body and what it means. I was able to view the remains video footage in Frederick Shannon's studio. My comments are based on that observation.

The obvious theory would conclude that at least one member of the crew "knew" the FITZGERALD was sinking or was worried enough to don a life jacket, an extremely unusual occurrence on a freighter.

From the position of the cork panels, apparently the jacket was not tied off in front, thus implying great haste, a lack of time or just confusion.

The crewman didn't float because he was released at a depth below which cork, due to the extreme pressure of the water, doesn't float. Perhaps he was dragged to this depth by the suction of the forward half as it dove for the bottom. Or, maybe he was caught on a piece of the ship and pulled down until the bow's impact knocked him free below the "no float depth" for cork. As a third alternative, he could have been in the ship and ejected by the force of the bottom impact. Because the bacteria that forms the gases necessary for the body to float can't grow in water as cold as that at the bottom of the lake, it simply remained where it landed. Now it is a silent sentinel guarding the EDMUND FITZGERALD, the pride of the fleet.

There is another theory to the body, namely that it may not even be from FITZGERALD! There is after all, no hard evidence linking it to the wreck. It was found near the wreck but not in it. The generally deteriorated condition, including clothing, does not easily relate to FITZGERALD. The remains show evidence of having been clad perhaps, in coveralls, while the life jacket was made of heavier canvas. Virtually none of this material is still present. Just yards away, a canvas deck screen is resting on a rail and linen and wool blankets are visible in cabins. In a period as short as 19 years in icy waters at the bottom of Lake Superior, such material does not quickly disintegrate. This writer has handled clothing that has been submerged in much shallower and warmer water for over 65 years. The deterioration of the cloth associated with the FITZGERALD remains, is in my opinion, inconsistent with experience. The remains proper are also deteriorated beyond that expected with a mere 19 years submergence. Examples from other Lake Superior wrecks would suggest it should be more intact. If you accept the concept of FITZGERALD diving for the bottom at a very rapid rate, then the crew in the pilothouse would have been struck by a devastating wall of water coming through the forward windows and washed out the back of the house. The bodies should have been deposited in the area well to the stern of the forward section, and not as far forward as this one is.

There are principally four ways to identify a body.

A. Previous medical history in terms of bone structure, breaks and injuries.

B. Skin marks such as tattoos and finger prints.

C. Dental.

D. DNA testing.

Based on conditions in this instance the first method is largely irrelevant. The others require recovery and forensic work. Until (and if) such action happens, all we have is speculation. Nonetheless, until a positive identification is made, the only evidence linking it to the FITZGERALD is circumstantial.

If it isn't from FITZGERALD, then what is it from? It could be from a number of wrecks lost in the eastern Lake, including the French minesweepers INKERMAN and CERISOLES, lost in November 1918. Both vessels were downbound from Thunder Bay for the Soo when they sank in a terrific gale. Neither vessel has ever been found, nor a single body from the 36 man French naval crews recovered. It is believed by some researchers that the vessels could have made the eastern Lake before being over-

217

whelmed. It is possible therefore the remains are not from FITZGERALD, but instead one of the French sailors. At this point only the Lake knows. Tossed by the tempestuous seas and later locked in the winter ice, the French sailor drifted until he sank. Six decades later, in a cloud of silt, he was joined by FITZGERALD. Other possibilities could be crewmen from any of the Lake Superior wrecks. "Floaters" as they were popularly called, ranged over the entire Lake, regardless of where the vessel sank.

The cork life jacket can be explained easily. 75 years ago adherence to strict safety equipment standards were not always stringently enforced. The jackets could have been old, poorly maintained or in such condition that buoyancy was compromised. While the idea of the remains being from one of the minesweepers certainly is a long shot, it is none-the-less credible. Paraphrasing Winston Churchill's comment on Russia, FITZGERALD is truly an enigma wrapped in a riddle. We should not jump to conclusions without irrefutable proof.

The open door in the pilothouse may not be as significant as originally thought. Many masters made it a practice to always run with an open lee door, especially in thick weather. With a door open it was far easier to hear other vessels and keep a proper lookout. This was most critical when the radar was out or when blitzed by a snow squall, both conditions common to the FITZGERALD at 7:10 pm, November 10. It is just another FITZGERALD conundrum.

My personal thought is that such expeditions as we saw in 1994 should not continue. Unless a viable scientific purpose can be articulated, there is no valid reason for further diving activity. This is a change from my previous stance. The concerns of family members should be respected. Perhaps some day though, a scientific researcher will discover the true cause of the loss and finally solve one of the great mysteries of the Great Lakes. This would be a fitting tribute to the men of FITZGERALD.

EXPEDITION 95

At the request of the family members and with the permission of the vessel's owner and the Canadian government, FITZGERALD's bell was recovered by a special expedition on July 4, 1995. The group was under the direction of Dr. Joseph MacInnis, had the full support of the Great Lakes Shipwreck Historical Society, National Geographic Society and Canadian Navy. After conservation measures, the 200 pound, 22 inch bronze bell was placed in the Great Lakes Shipwreck Historical Society Museum at Whitefish Point as part of a FITZGERALD memorial.

The 245-foot HMCS CORMORANT, a Canadian Navy diving support vessel, provided surface operational support. The actual recovery was made by a diver using a high tech "Newt Suit," a self propelled armored diving suit. A replica bell, engraved with the names of FITZGERALD's crew, was respectfully replaced on the wreck.

On July 7th, the newly recovered bell was formally presented to the families by the Canadian government during a very moving ceremony in the American Soo. Once the inevitable speeches were finally over, the bell was rung 29 times, once for each man lost and once more in tribute to all sailors perished on the lakes. As they were able, a family member rang the bell as each man's name was read. Volunteers from the CORMORANT did this most honorable duty when a family member was unavailable.

The single theme strongly stressed by several speakers, including representatives of the Canadian government, was the need to close the wreck to future diving activity. Unless a strong scientific argument could be made, needless exploitation should cease.

The bell was an important symbol for family members. Representing the "soul" of the ship, it's recovery and subsequent placement as a memorial helps to put the tragedy to rest. For many it's a type of closure.

The FITZGERALD memorial at Whitefish Point also speaks directly to the heart of the Great Lakes maritime community. Honoring not only the "good ship and crew," but also all the sailors who ever meet death on the lakes, past, present and future.

Fred Shannon, the organizer of one of the 1994 expeditions, attempted to stop the bell recovery. In May 1995 he sued in an Ingham County, Michigan court. The case was dismissed after the judge ruled he had no legal standing to block the effort.

Since FITZGERALD went to the bottom, the experts knew someday a diver would reach her; not a man in an armored suit or mini-sub, but an actual free swimming diver. In the 1995 version (fourth edition, 19th printing) of this book I stated, "It is only a matter of time before the first diver reaches the wreck using an exotic gas mixture." On September 1, 1995, two men, Michael Zee of Chicago and Terrance Tyall of Orlando did reach FITZGERALD. Randy Sullivan of Soo, Canada provided critical surface support. The dive, taking nearly three hours, was made using a special gas mixture of oxygen, helium and nitrogen in six different combinations. Bottom time was a bare twelve minutes, with four minutes on the wreck itself and eight in descent. The rest of the time was spent in assent. This was undoubtedly the deepest "free" dive in Great Lakes history and it was done for much the same reason men climb Mount Everest - for the challenge.

It is my conclusion that since the FITZGERALD has become an integral part of the legend of the Great Lakes, she will continue to hold a position of fascination to the Lakes community. The memorabilia will continue and we will inevitably see additional video work, both ROV and manned submersible. Whether anything in the future will ever answer the questions concerning her loss remains highly speculative.

As Gordon Lightfoot so aptly stated in his wonderful ballad, "the legend lives on. . ."

THE WRECK OF THE
EDMUND FITZGERALD

Lyrics by Gordon Lightfoot

Reprinted with permission from Moose Music Ltd.

The legend lives on from the Chippewa on down
of the big lake they called Gitche Gumee
The lake it is said never gives up her dead
when the skies of November turn gloomy
With a load of iron ore 26,000 tons more
than the Edmund Fitzgerald weighed empty
that good ship and true was a bone to be chewed
when the gales of November came early

The ship was the pride of the American side
comin' back from some mill in Wisconsin
As the big freighters go it was bigger than most
with a crew and good captain well seasoned
concluding some terms with a couple of steel firms
when they left fully loaded for Cleveland
and late that night when the ship's bell rang
could it be the north wind they'd bin feelin'

The wind in the wires made a tattletale sound
and a wave broke over the railing
and every man knew as the captain did too
twas the witch of November come stealin'
The dawn came late and the breakfast had to wait
when the gales of November came slashin'
When afternoon came it was freezin' rain
in the face of a hurricane west wind

When suppertime came the old cook came on deck
sayin' "fellas it's too rough to feed ya"
At seven p.m. a main hatchway caved in
he said "fellas it's bin good to know ya"

221

The captain wired in he had water comin' in
and the good ship and crew was in peril
and later that night when 'is lights went out of sight
came the wreck of the Edmund Fitzgerald

Does anyone know where the love of god goes
when the waves turn the minutes to hours?
The searchers all say they'd have made Whitefish Bay
if they'd put fifteen more miles behind 'em
They might have split up or they might have capsized
they may have broke deep and took water
and all that remains is the faces and the names
of the wives and the sons and the daughters

Lake Huron rolls Superior sings
in the rooms of her ice water mansion
Old Michigan steams like a young man's
dreams the islands and bays are for sportsmen
and farther below Lake Ontario
takes in what Lake Erie can send her
and the iron boats go as the mariners all know
with the gales of November remembered

In a musty old hall in Detroit they prayed
in the maritime sailors' cathedral
the church bell chimed 'til it rang 29 times
for each man on the Edmund Fitzgerald
The legend lives on from the Chippewa on down
of the big lake they called Gitche Gumee
Superior they said never gives up her dead
when the gales of November come early

The FITZGERALD continues to tantalize. It is evident neither her legend or attraction will die.

RECORD OF MISSING CREWMEN

The following crewmembers are missing:

McSORLEY, Ernest M.
Master
Toledo, OH

McCARTHY, John H.
First Mate
Bay Village, OH

PRATT, James A.
Second Mate
Lakewood, OH

ARMAGOST, Michael E.
Third Mate
Iron River, WI

HOLL, George J.
Chief Engineer
Cabot, PA

BINDON, Edward F.
First Asst. Engineer
Fairport Harbor, OH

EDWARDS, Thomas E.
Second Asst. Engineer
Oregon, OH

BEETCHER, Frederick J.
Porter
Superior, WI

BENTSEN, Thomas
Oiler
St Joseph, MI

BORGESON, Thomas D.
AB Maintenance Man
Duluth, MN

CHURCH, Nolan F.
Porter
Silver Bay, MN

CUNDY, Ransom E.
Watchman
Superior, WI

HUDSON, Bruce L.
Deckhand
N. Olmsted, OH

KALMON, Allen G.
Second Cook
Washburn, WI

HASKELL, Russell G.
Second Asst. Engineer
Millbury, OH

MacLELLAN, Gordon F.
Wiper
Clearwater, FL

CHAMPEAU, Oliver J.
Third Asst. Engineer
Milwaukee, WI

MAZES, Joseph W.
Special Maintenance Man
Ashland, WI

O'BRIEN, Eugene W.
Wheelsman
St. Paul, MN

SPENGLER, William J.
Watchman
Toledo, OH

PECKOL, Karl A.
Watchman
Ashtabula, OH

THOMAS, Mark A.
Deckhand
Richmond Hts., OH

POVIACH, John J.
Wheelsman
Bradenton, FL

WALTON, Ralph G.
Oiler
Fremont, OH

RAFFERTY, Robert C.
Steward
Toledo, OH

WEISS, David E.
Cadet (Deck)
Agoura, CA

RIIPPA, Paul M.
Deckhand
Ashtabula, OH

WILHELM, Blaine H.
Oiler
Moquah, WI

SIMMONS, John D.
Wheelsman
Ashland, WI

BIBLIOGRAPHY

Boyer, Dwight. *Ships and Men of the Great Lakes,* New Dodd, Mead & Co., 1977.

Greenwood, John O., and Dills, Michael. *Greenwood's and Dill's Lake Boats '73.* Cleveland, Ohio, Freshwater Press, 1973.

O'Brien, T. Michael. *Guardians of the Eighth Sea, A History of the U.S. Coast Guard on the Great Lakes.* Washington, D.C., U.S. Government Printing Office, 1976.

Ratigan, William. *Great Lakes Shipwrecks and Survivals.* Grand Rapids, Michigan, Wm. B. Eerdmans Publishing Company, 1977.

Shannon, Frederick J. *Expedition 94 — Official Report,* Mt. Moris, Michigan, 1994.

Trimble, Paul E., Vice Admiral USCG (Ret.). "Year-round Navigation on the Great Lakes." *Inland Seas,* Winter, 1976, pp. 248-254.

Wolff, Julius F. "In Retrospect." *Inland Seas,* Summer 1976, pp. 122-124.

Wolff, Julius F. "One Hundred Years of the Coast Guard on Lake Superior." *Inland Seas,* Spring 1976, pp. 40-51.

Sundstrom, E.S. "And Suddenly She's Gone." *Michigan Travelogue,* November, 1976, pp. 22-29.

Nor'Easter, Vol. 1, No. 1, Sept.—Oct., 1976.

U.S. Congress House Committee on Merchant Marine and Fisheries. *Coast Guard Activities In The Upper Great Lakes, Hearings* before the Subcommittee on Coast Guard and Navigation, House of Representatives, 94th Cong., July 16,1976. U.S. Department of Transportation, U.S. Coast Guard, *Summary of Results of Survey of Wreckage of Edmund Fitzgerald.*

U.S. Department of Transportation, *Marine Board of Investigation, S.S. Daniel J. Morrell Sinking with Loss of Life, Lake Huron, 29 November 1966. U.S. Coast Guard Marine Board of Investigation Report and Commandant's Action.* Released 4 March 1968.

U.S. Department of Transportation, *Marine Casualty Report, S.S. Edmund Fitzgerald; Sinking in Lake Superior on 10 November 1975 with Loss of Life, U.S. Coast Guard Marine Board of Investigation Report and Commandant's Action.* 26 July 1977.

U.S. Department of Transportation, U.S. Coast Guard, *Merchant Vessels of the United States* (various issues). Washington, D.C., Government Printing Office.

Plain Dealer, Cleveland, Ohio November 9, 12 & 15, 1975.

Detroit News, Detroit, Michigan, November 10, 1975.

International Defense Review, February, 1993.

Marquette Mining Journal, Marquette, Michigan, November 12, 13, 14, 19, 21 & 22 December 13, 1975 November 11 & 26, December 31, 1976, September 29, November 6, 1977.

Milwaukee Journal, Milwaukee, Wisconsin, November 12 & 13, 1975, August 3, September 30,1977.

Sault Evening News, Sault Ste. Marie, Michigan, November 11, 1975, May 20 & 21, 1976.

Correspondence, Lake Carriers' Association to National Transportation Safety Board, dated September 16, 1977, November 3, 1977.

Correspondence, Public Affairs Officer, Ninth Coast Guard District, to Author, December 28, 1976, October 3, 1977.

Correspondence, Recorder, Marine Board of Investigation to Author, 25 July 1977.

Correspondence, Seaward, Inc., to Author, 24 June 1977.

A GLOSSARY OF NAUTICAL TERMS

AFT— Of or near the rear or the stern of the vessel.

AGROUND— On the bottom of a body of water.

ANEMOMETER— A wind gauge. Cups are set vertically on horizontal arms and are set in motion by the wind. Velocity of the wind is measured by the revolutions of a vertical shaft.

ASTERN— Behind the vessel, to the rear or backwards.

BALLAST— Any heavy substance laid in the hold of a vessel to steady it. A vessel sails "in ballast" when she carries no cargo.

BALLAST TANKS— Tanks in the lower holds of a vessel which carry water (and sometimes oil). They can be pumped out and flooded at will to stabilize the ship.

BARGE— A flat-bottomed freight boat for harbors or inland waters. Often a large towing vessel.

BEACON— (See RADIO BEACON)

BOW THRUSTER — A propeller installed in a steamer's bow below the waterline. It offers maneuverability about the docks and often eliminates the need for tug assistance in harbors.

BROADSIDE—The side of a vessel above the waterline.

BULKHEAD— An upright partition in a vessel separating compartments.

BUOY— A warning float moored on a dangerous rock or shoal or at the edge of a channel.

CANDLE POWER— A unit of the luminous intensity of light arrived at by national agreement.

CHANNEL— The deep part of a river, harbor, etc., Also a navigable passage between the shallower parts.

COAMING— A structure or curb about a hatchway to keep water from entering.

FATHOM— Six feet of depth in water.

FATHOMETER—A sonic device to measure depth.

FLOTSAM— Floating wreckage or goods.

FORWARD— Towards the front or bow of a ship.

FOUNDER—To sink after filling with water.

GALE— A continuous wind blowing stronger than a stiff breeze; Varies in velocity from 34 to 63 knots.

GREEN WATER (or GREEN SEA)— Solid water shipped aboard (as opposed to spray).

HAND LEAD—A 7- or 14-pound lead attached to a line for manual sounding.

HATCH— An opening in the deck of the ship giving access to spaces beneath. "Hatch" is also used to mean "hatch cover."

HATCH COVER— Heavy sections of planking or steel that cover the hatch opening.

HOLD— The space below the decks of a vessel where cargo is stored.

HULL— The body of a ship, exclusive of the masts, sails, yards and rigging.

KNOT— Speed of a nautical mile in an hour, equivalent to 1.15 statute miles an hour.

LEE— Place or side sheltered from the wind.

LIST— The leaning of a vessel to one side.

MASTER— Commander of a merchant vessel.

NORTHER— A gale or storm from the north.

PILOT— Navigator.

PILOTHOUSE — (also WHEELHOUSE) Room under or on the bridge where steering wheel is located.

RADIO BEACON— A radio station on shore which sends an assigned signal for bearing-taking.

SEAWAY— A way or lane over the sea; or the motion of the sea when clear of shoal water.

SHOAL— A shallow place in a body of water.

SPAR DECK—The upper deck of a ship.

STARBOARD— Looking forward, the right side of a vessel.

ABOUT THE AUTHOR

Frederick Stonehouse holds a Master of Arts Degree in History from Northern Michigan University, Marquette, Michigan, and has authored twelve books on Great Lakes vessel losses. *Isle Royale Shipwrecks, Went Missing, Munising Shipwrecks, Lake Superior's "Shipwreck Coast"* and *Keweenaw Shipwrecks* are all published by Avery Color Studios.

He has also been a consultant for both the U.S. National Park Service and Parks Canada.

His articles have been published in *Skin Diver, Lake Superior Magazine, Michigan History* and *Diver* Magazines. He has been a member of the Great Lakes Historical and Marquette County Historical Societies, the Lake Superior Marine Museum Association, the Alger Underwater Preserve Committee and a member of the Board of Directors of the Marquette Maritime Museum.

Stonehouse makes his home in Flushing, Michigan.

PLEASE RETURN TO:

P.O. Box 308
Marquette MI 49855

CALL TOLL FREE
1-800-722-9925

Your complete shipping address:

_____

_____

_____

_____

Fold, Staple, Affix Stamp and Mail

- -

_____

_____

_____

_____

P.O. Box 308
Marquette MI 49855